MYTHS

Judy L. Paris
Sandra D. Cheney

Butte Publications, Inc.

MYTHS

Judy L. Paris and Sandra D. Cheney

Editor: Jane Van Dusen
Cover Design and Page Layout: Anita Jones
Cover Illustration: Merry Ann McGlinn
Illustrators: Merry Ann McGlinn, Diana Bennett, and Justin B. Paris

Butte Publications, Inc.
P.O. Box 1328
Hillsboro, OR 97123-1328
USA

ISBN 1-884362-47-8

Dedication

To new beginnings…
and to dreams come true

JLP/SDC

Introduction to the Teacher

Myths provides students with the opportunity to share in the cultural heritage of the Greek and Roman people. Twenty myths are retold so that students can fully appreciate the Greek and Roman beliefs without the barriers of complicated syntactic structures.

Additional stories and activities explain the mythological origins of the modern calendar, modern symbols, and the names of the planets and other celestial bodies. These stories and activities afford an excellent opportunity for students to learn how the mythology of the ancient Greeks and Romans is integral to our present-day culture. This book provides opportunities throughout for cross-curricular study in science, social studies, art, and history while strengthening language skills.

ORGANIZATION

Myths is divided into six sections. In each section, glossaries provide simple definitions of vocabulary used in the text. Study questions throughout each section, cumulative evaluations at the end of the four central sections, and enrichment activities enhance students' interest in and comprehension of the material.

The sections in this book are numbered with Roman numerals. You may wish to introduce students to the system of Roman numerals before introducing the material in Section I.

SECTION I: AN INTRODUCTION TO GREEK AND ROMAN MYTHS

Section I provides a short explanation of what the Greeks and Romans believed about their gods and goddesses, explains what myths are, and describes the importance of Mount Olympus. The study questions that follow these explanations evaluate the students' comprehension of the material.

A list of the well-known gods and goddesses gives their Greek and Roman names and tells their primary responsibilities. A brief biographical sketch of each important deity reinforces and expands the information in the list. A crossword puzzle of the gods and goddesses focuses the students' attention on spelling the names of the gods and goddesses. Study questions evaluate the students' understanding of the individual gods and goddesses.

SECTIONS II, III, IV, AND V: THE MYTHS

Each of these sections includes five myths written using simple linguistic structures and appropriate vocabulary. The glossaries that preface each section give simple definitions for vocabulary that may not be familiar to students. The study questions that follow each myth evaluate the students' comprehension of the vocabulary and characters in the myth, the sequence of events, and the story development.

Each section ends with a section evaluation which is a cumulative test of the students' comprehension of all five myths, including the vocabulary, plot, and characters of each myth.

SECTION VI: MYTHOLOGY IN MODERN TIMES

Using Mythology Today, the first part of this section, introduces students to the concept that ideas and words from ancient times are still used today and that by studying mythology, they will broaden their knowledge of the world around them. Included in this part are a glossary, an explanation of concepts (*Mythology in Our Daily Lives*), information about the months of the year and the derivation of their names, and study questions which test the students' comprehension of the material.

Symbol Stories provide students with examples of the application of Greek and Roman mythology in everyday life. Each story explains how a common symbol in modern society is derived from a Greek or Roman myth. This segment of Section VI also includes a glossary and study questions testing the students' comprehension of the material.

The Solar System and the Planets explains how mythology is used in science, particularly the study of our solar system and galaxy. This segment includes a glossary; an explanation of the relationships between planets, stars, and other celestial bodies (*Our Galaxy and Our Solar System*); a story about each of the nine planets; and study questions which test the students' comprehension of the material.

Using Your Resources gives students an awareness of all the people and things around them that can help them get information. *Solar System Graphic* helps students utilize various resources to label a graphic of the solar system. *Planets, Gods and Goddesses, and Symbols* helps students gain a clearer understanding of symbols, how they can be used, and why we use them. It is also a creative activity that will give students an opportunity to think of their own ideas for symbols.

The final portion of Section VI suggests some additional enrichment activities so that students may expand their knowledge of mythology and symbols. The activities that are included encourage students to pursue in depth some of the topics briefly discussed in this section (businesses, organizations, symbols, and scientific concepts).

ANSWER KEY

An answer key for the crossword puzzle, study questions, section evaluations, and the activities in *Using Your Resources* is included at the back of the book. The answer key may or may not be made available to the students at your discretion.

PROCEDURES

While you are encouraged to adapt this material creatively to any situation, the following order of proceeding through the book is suggested:

1. Have the students read the glossary for Section I, *An Introduction to Greek and Roman Myths.*

2. Have the students read *Greek and Roman Beliefs* and *Mount Olympus* and complete the accompanying study questions.

3. Have the students read the *List of Greek and Roman Gods and Goddesses* and complete the accompanying study questions.

4. Have the students read the biographical sketches, *Important Gods and Goddesses,* and complete the accompanying study questions.

5. Have the students read the glossary for the first myth in Section II.

6. Have the students read the first myth in Section II and then complete the study questions following it.

7. Repeat steps 5 and 6 for the other four myths in Section II.

8. After completing the five myths and their study questions, the students should work through the evaluation for Section II.

9. Repeat steps 5 through 8 for Sections III, IV, and V.

10. In Section VI, under *Using Mythology Today*, have the students read the glossary and *Mythology in Our Daily Lives*. Then have the students read *The Months* and complete the information in the accompanying study questions.

11. In Section VI, under *Symbol Stories,* have the students read the glossary, *Mythological Symbols*, and the five symbol stories. Then have them complete the study questions.

12. In Section VI, under *The Solar System and the Planets*, have the students read the glossary and *Our Galaxy and Our Solar System*. Then have the students read the nine planet stories and complete the accompanying study questions.

13. Have the students read the introduction to *Using Your Resources* and complete the *Solar System Graphic*.

14. Under *Using Your Resources*, have the students complete *Planets, Gods and Goddesses, and Symbols*. Encourage them to use their creativity in thinking of new symbols to represent the gods and goddesses.

15. Have the students attempt one or more of the enrichment activities at the end of Section VI.

GENERAL ENRICHMENT ACTIVITIES

To supplement the stories and exercises in this book, you may direct students to do the following activities or you may design other activities to suit students' specific needs and abilities.

1. Learn the basic symbols for Roman numerals and develop math problems for the class.

2. Create a mask of a mythological character.

3. Rewrite a myth so that it takes place in the present.

4. Pretend you are a television talk show host and another student is a mythological character. Interview the mythological character and ask questions about his or her life.

5. Imagine that you have found a time capsule from the Greeks or Romans. Describe each object that you find in the capsule and explain its purpose in the capsule.

6. Write a biographical sketch of a mythological character.

7. Create a piece of art that relates to a myth. Use available materials such as nuts and bolts, sequins, and glitter, and mount them on wood or heavy tag board.

8. Construct a diorama that relates to a myth.

9. Choose an object. Pretend that you are the god or goddess who controls that object and explain your powers.

10. Make a bauble relating to a god, a goddess, or a person from a myth. A bauble consists of eight paper circles. Fold the sides of each circle to form a triangle in the center. Staple or glue the circles together at their three folded edges, creating an eight-sided ornament that can be suspended from the ceiling of the classroom. Put pictures or drawings on each of the eight triangular sections of the bauble.

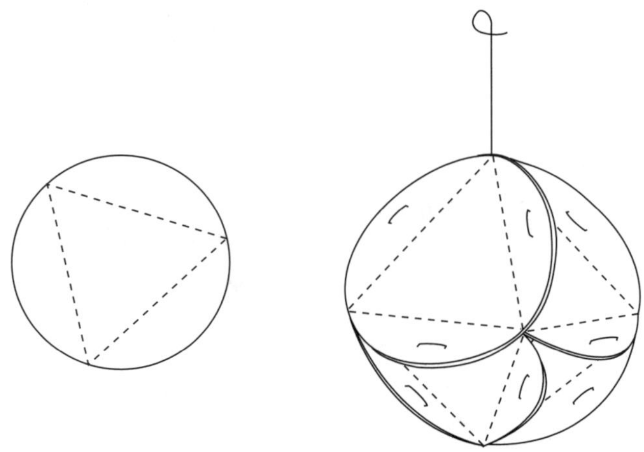

11. Choose an emotion or an object in nature. Invent your own myth about how that emotion or object came to be.

12. Look in your library for information on Greek or Roman customs, costumes, or foods. Prepare a booklet with the information you find.

13. Imagine you are a god or goddess living in this century. Explain one event in your life.

14. Make a family tree of gods and goddesses.

15. Make a poster advertising a god or goddess as a guest speaker at your school.

16. Gather five cartoons, advertisements, pictures, or articles that relate to mythology from magazines or newspapers. Create a bulletin board display with your clippings.

17. Collect five objects that relate to mythology and explain to the class why each one was important to the Greeks or Romans.

18. Come to class in costume as a god or goddess. Lecture to the class about yourself.

19. Act out a myth. Videotape the performance.

CONTENTS

SECTION I

AN INTRODUCTION TO GREEK AND ROMAN MYTHS

GLOSSARY

1. afraid	scared
2. ancient	very old
3. to control (controlled)	to manage; to take care of
4. crops	plants grown for food
5. to discuss (discussed)	to talk about
6. earth	the land on which people live
7. emotions	feelings
8. to explain (explained)	to tell the meaning of
9. god	a male character that looks like a person and can do magic things; people worshipped many gods
10. goddess	a female god
11. lesson	something that will help your life
12. mountain	a large hill
13. nature	everything in the world that people did not make
14. to obey (obeyed)	to do what someone tells you to do
15. permission	allowing someone to do something
16. pleased	happy; satisfied
17. problems	things that happen that are difficult to take care of
18. to punish (punished)	to cause someone pain for doing something wrong
19. to reward (rewarded)	to give something nice for doing something good
20. to understand	to know about something
21. world	earth

GREEK AND ROMAN BELIEFS

The people who lived in Greece and Rome in ancient times wanted to explain the things they did not understand in the world. They were curious about nature, emotions, and many other things in their lives. They had many questions, such as: What makes the thunder in the sky?, Why does summer change to fall?, and Why do people fall in love? Since they did not know much about science and research, they could not find answers to their questions. Sometimes they were afraid because they could not explain many things.

The Greek and Roman people did not believe in one god. The Greeks and Romans believed that many gods and goddesses controlled the things they did not understand. Each god and goddess had special work to do. The people thought one god controlled the sea, one goddess controlled the plants, one god controlled love, and one goddess controlled beauty.

The Greek and Roman people wrote many stories about the gods and goddesses. People, animals, and unusual creatures were also characters in some of the stories. One of the unusual creatures looked like a dog with three heads and another was half man and half goat. The stories were called myths. The myths explained many things that people did not understand. Some myths told about people's emotions. Some myths explained about nature. Some myths taught people lessons. The Greek and Roman people thought that the stories were true.

Now we know that the stories are not true. Science and research can explain much of what the Greek and Roman people did not understand. We also know that gods and goddesses do not control our lives. Today people read myths because they are interesting and entertaining stories. Reading myths is also a good way to learn about the Greeks and the Romans and their beliefs.

MOUNT OLYMPUS

The Greek and Roman people believed that Mount Olympus was a very high mountain. Clouds covered the top of the mountain. The Greek and Roman people thought that the god Jupiter and the goddess Juno lived on Mount Olympus. They also thought the other gods and goddesses visited Mount Olympus often.

The Greek and Roman people believed that sometimes gods and goddesses had meetings on Mount Olympus. During the meetings, they talked about themselves and the people on earth. They discussed problems, made plans to help people on earth and talked about ways to help each other.

When the people on earth did good things, the gods and goddesses were happy and rewarded them. Sometimes they rewarded the people by helping them to win wars and by making their crops grow better. When the people on earth did bad things, the gods and goddesses became angry and punished them. Sometimes they punished them by causing storms and floods, by changing people into animals, and by destroying crops. Sometimes the gods and goddesses had parties on Mount Olympus. They relaxed and had fun.

The Greek and Roman people also believed that people were not allowed to go to Mount Olympus. If people went to Mount Olympus without permission, the gods and goddesses became angry and punished them. If people obeyed the gods and goddesses and stayed away from Mount Olympus, the gods and goddesses were pleased. Then the gods and goddesses did good things for the people on earth.

GREEK AND ROMAN BELIEFS and MOUNT OLYMPUS STUDY QUESTIONS

Read each sentence. Write the correct answer in each blank.

1. The Greek and Roman people believed in ______________________________.

   a. no gods b. many gods c. one god

2. The Greek and Roman people wrote stories that were called ______________________.

   a. lessons b. gods c. myths

3. The Greek and Roman people thought their stories were ______________________.

   a. true b. not true c. false

4. Some myths explained about ______________________________.

   a. emotions and nature b. stories and songs c. work and play

5. The Greek and Roman people thought each god and goddess ______________________ something special.

   a. covered b. controlled c. fought

6. The gods and goddesses lived on ______________________________.

   a. Mount Greece b. Mount Rome c. Mount Olympus

7. The gods and goddesses ______________________ the people when they did good things.

   a. rewarded b. punished c. explained

8. The gods and goddesses punished people who went to Mount Olympus without ______________

   ____.

   a. emotions b. clouds c. permission

9. The gods and goddesses ______________________ the people when they did bad things.

   a. rewarded b. punished c. explained

10. The gods and goddesses had ______________________________ on Mount Olympus.

    a. parties and meetings b. crops and floods c. lessons and stories

LIST OF GODS AND GODDESSES

Each god and goddess had two names, a Roman name and a Greek name. Today, the Roman name is used more often than the Greek name.

Roman Name	Greek Name	What the God or Goddess Controlled
Jupiter	Zeus	king of the gods and goddesses and the sky
Juno	Hera	queen of the gods and goddesses
Pluto	Hades	king of Hades (the underworld or the kingdom of the dead)
Proserpina	Persephone	queen of Hades
Neptune	Poseidon	god of the sea
Ceres	Demeter	goddess of the harvest
Apollo	Apollo	god of music, poetry, and the sun
Venus	Aphrodite	goddess of love and beauty
Mercury	Hermes	god of speed; messenger of the gods
Hercules	Heracles	god of strength
Cupid	Eros	god of love
Vesta	Hestia	goddess of the hearth or home
Minerva	Athena	goddess of wisdom and courage
Diana	Artemis	goddess of the moon and hunting
Mars	Ares	god of war
Vulcan	Hephaestus	god of fire and metal
Juventas	Hebe	goddess of youth
Bacchus	Dionysus	god of wine
Saturn	Cronus	god of time and agriculture

LIST OF GODS AND GODDESSES
STUDY QUESTIONS

*Read each sentence. Then fill in each blank with the word **Greek** or the word **Roman**.*

1. Venus is the ____________________ name for the goddess of love.

2. Ares is the ____________________ name for the god of war.

3. Vulcan is the ____________________ name and Hephaestus is the ____________________ name for the god of fire.

4. Poseidon is the ____________________ name for the god of the sea.

5. Jupiter is the ____________________ name for the king of the gods and goddesses.

6. Bacchus is the ____________________ name for the god of wine.

7. Eros is the ____________________ name and Cupid is the ____________________ name for the god of love.

8. Ceres is the ____________________ name for the goddess of the harvest.

9. Hera is the ____________________ name and Juno is the ____________________ name for the queen of the gods and goddesses.

10. Minerva is the ____________________ name for the goddess of wisdom.

11. Proserpina is the ____________________ name and Persephone is the ____________________ name for the queen of Hades.

12. Mercury is the ____________________ name for the god of speed.

13. Pluto is the ____________________ name and Hades is the ____________________ name for the king of the underworld.

14. Artemis is the ____________________ name and Diana is the ____________________ name for the goddess of the moon and hunting.

15. Saturn is the ____________________ name for the god of time and agriculture.

16. Hebe is the ____________________ name for the goddess of youth.

17. Apollo is the ____________________ name and Apollo is the ____________________ name for the god of the sun.

IMPORTANT GODS AND GODDESSES

JUPITER or ZEUS

Jupiter was the king of the gods and goddesses. He was the ruler of the sky and the earth. He was the most important and most powerful god. He was also wise and made good laws. When Jupiter was angry with people, he used thunder and lightning as weapons to punish them. Although Jupiter was married to Juno, he often fell in love with other goddesses and women on earth. He had many children.

JUNO or HERA

Juno was the wife of Jupiter and queen of the gods and goddesses. She ruled the sky and the earth with Jupiter. She was very beautiful and the most important goddess. Her favorite animal was the peacock. She was also the goddess of marriage. Jupiter and Juno had a difficult marriage because Jupiter often fell in love with other goddesses and women on earth. Juno was very jealous and often became unhappy. Sometimes she punished the women that Jupiter loved

NEPTUNE or POSEIDON

Neptune was the god of the sea. He ruled all of the things in the sea. He rode in a chariot pulled by sea creatures and carried a trident. A trident is a three-pronged spear that he sometimes threw at enemies. He was also called the earthshaker because people thought he caused earthquakes. The Greek and Roman people loved the sea and liked Neptune very much.

CERES or DEMETER

Ceres was the goddess of the harvest. She controlled the seasons and all of the plants on earth. The Greek and Roman people believed that Ceres helped their crops to grow better. Proserpina was the daughter of Ceres. The people liked Ceres very much.

PLUTO or HADES

Pluto was the king of Hades, which was also called the underworld. Hades was the place where the spirits of the dead were sent. The Greek and Roman people loved life. They did not want to think about death, so they did not honor Pluto. Many of the people feared Pluto because he was not a friendly god.

APOLLO or APOLLO

Apollo was the god of the sun. The Greek and Roman people believed that Apollo drove a large chariot across the sky everyday. He carried the sun in his chariot. Apollo was also the god of music and poetry. He was an excellent athlete and skillful with the bow and arrow. Many young men honored Apollo, so they studied music, poetry, and sports. Apollo fell in love often, but never married.

VENUS or APHRODITE

Venus was the goddess of love and beauty. She was the most beautiful goddess and many gods and men on earth loved her. Venus was married to Vulcan, the god of fire. They had a son named Cupid who was the god of love. Her favorite bird was the dove.

MERCURY or HERMES

Mercury was the god of speed and the messenger of the gods and goddesses. He also protected travelers and merchants. Mercury had wings on his cap and on his sandals. The wings helped him to run fast. Mercury's most important duty was to lead the souls of the dead from the earth to Hades.

HERCULES or HERACLES

Hercules was the son of Jupiter and Juno. He was a very strong man who lived on earth. Hercules had to perform twelve labors to become a god. The gods and goddesses thought that Hercules performed his labors very well. After Hercules lived on earth for a long time, he became the god of strength.

CUPID or EROS

Cupid was the god of love. Sometimes Cupid was nice and other times he was mean. He was a very cute god who had wings on his back. He always carried a bow and some arrows. Some of the arrows caused people to fall in love and some of the arrows caused people to hate each other. Cupid often played tricks on people and the other gods and goddesses. He was the son of Venus and Vulcan.

PROSERPINA or PERSEPHONE

Proserpina was the lovely daughter of Ceres and Jupiter. Pluto, the king of Hades, brought Proserpina to Hades to live with him. She became the queen of Hades. Proserpina did not like Hades and missed her mother very much. Proserpina spent six months of each year in Hades and six months of each year with her mother on earth.

SATURN or CRONUS

Saturn was the first king of the gods and goddesses. He had six children. One of his children was Jupiter. Saturn was mean to his children. When the children became older, they punished their father and forced him to leave the throne. Then Jupiter became the king of the gods and goddesses. Saturn was the god of time and agriculture.

DIANA or ARTEMIS

Diana was the goddess of the moon and hunting. She was the daughter of Jupiter and twin sister of Apollo. She enjoyed hunting in the woods and was skillful with a bow and arrow. Diana never fell in love or married.

MARS or ARES

Mars was the god of war. He was a son of Jupiter and Juno. He was very strong and liked to cause trouble. Mars liked many women on earth and had many mean children. Some Greeks and Romans feared Mars, but some of them thought he was a coward. His favorite animal was the wolf.

BACCHUS or DIONYSUS

Bacchus was the god of wine and was a son of Jupiter. He protected the vineyards and the grape harvest. He brought joy and pleasure to many people. Bacchus wanted people to be happy and have many parties. His friends were satyrs and centaurs. Satyrs were half human and half goat. Centaurs were half human and half horse. Bacchus wore a purple robe and panthers pulled his chariot.

VULCAN or HEPHAESTUS

Vulcan was the god of fire and metal. He was the blacksmith for the gods and goddesses. He made weapons and armor for them. Vulcan worked in a volcano. When his forge became too hot, or he became angry, the volcano would erupt. Venus was his wife and Cupid was his son. The other gods and goddesses and the people on earth loved him because he was kind.

MINERVA or ATHENA

Minerva was the goddess of wisdom and courage. She was the favorite daughter of Jupiter. She was patient and wise. Minerva was a good warrior. She invented the war chariot and the horse bridle. She also gave the olive tree to the people on earth. Minerva never fell in love or married. Her favorite bird was the owl. Now we use the phrase "wise as an owl" to describe someone who is intelligent.

VESTA or HESTIA

Vesta was the goddess of the hearth and the home. She was a daughter of Saturn and a sister of Jupiter. Vesta never married. She protected the homes of Greek and Roman people. Vesta's job on Mount Olympus was to keep a fire lit in the palace of the gods and goddesses. Many Greek and Roman cities kept a fire burning in the center of the towns to honor Vesta. The people thought that the fire would protect their cities.

JUVENTAS or HEBE

Juventas was the goddess of youth. She was a daughter of Jupiter and was married to Hercules. She had the power to make old people young again. Her job on Mount Olympus was to serve nectar at the banquets of the gods and goddesses.

IMPORTANT GODS AND GODDESSES
STUDY QUESTIONS

Read each sentence and find the answer that completes the sentence correctly. Check the correct answer.

1. Many Greek and Roman people did not worship Pluto ______________________________.

   ______ a. because they did not want to think about death
   ______ b. because they loved death
   ______ c. because they liked spirits

2. Hercules became a god ____.

   ______ a. because he was a strong man
   ______ b. because he was the son of Jupiter
   ______ c. because he performed twelve labors

3. ______________________ was the twin sister of Apollo.

   ______ a. Juventas
   ______ b. Diana
   ______ c. Venus

4. Sometimes Cupid _________________________ on people and other gods.

   ______ a. told stories
   ______ b. played tricks
   ______ c. gave wings

5. Apollo carried the _________________ in his large chariot.

   ______ a. music
   ______ b. poetry
   ______ c. sun

6. Vesta ____________________ the homes of the Greek and Roman people.

   ______ a. pulled
   ______ b. feared
   ______ c. protected

7. Neptune threw his ________________________ at his enemies.

   ______ a. trident
   ______ b. earthquake
   ______ c. sea

8. Bacchus had a ______________________ pulled by panthers.

   ______ a. chair
   ______ b. chariot
   ______ c. chore

9. Jupiter's weapons were ______________________________.

______ a. sky and earth
______ b. thunder and lightning
______ c. king and people

10. Venus and Vulcan had a son named ____________________.

______ a. Cupid
______ b. Aphrodite
______ c. Apollo

11. Juventas was a goddess who was married to ____________________.

______ a. Hercules
______ b. Jupiter
______ c. Apollo

12. Saturn was the first king of the gods and goddesses and the ______________ of Jupiter.

______ a. uncle
______ b. brother
______ c. father

13. Proserpina was the _______________ of Ceres.

______ a. king
______ b. queen
______ c. daughter

14. The favorite animal of Mars was the ______________.

______ a. lion
______ b. wolf
______ c. tiger

15. Minerva gave the ___________ tree to the people on earth.

______ a. olive
______ b. grape
______ c. oak

16. Juno was jealous of some women on earth so __________________________.

______ a. she loved them
______ b. she punished them
______ c. she made them beautiful

17. Mercury had wings on his _______________________.

______ a. cap and sandals
______ b. souls and gods
______ c. duty

18. The Greek and Roman people thought __________________ caused earthquakes.

_____ a. Jupiter
_____ b. Neptune
_____ c. Pluto

19. Vulcan worked in a __________________.

_____ a. factory
_____ b. mine
_____ c. volcano

20. The people liked Ceres because ______________________________________.

_____ a. she helped their crops grow
_____ b. she controlled everything on earth
_____ c. she believed the myths

21. Mercury led the ____________________________ to Hades.

_____ a. messenger of the gods
_____ b. wings of speed
_____ c. souls of the dead

22. Proserpina spent six months in Hades and six months on _____________________.

_____ a. earth
_____ b. Mount Olympus
_____ c. Ocean

23. Some Greek and Roman people feared Mars and some thought he was a ______________.

_____ a. chariot
_____ b. centaur
_____ c. coward

24. ________________________ was the most important and the most powerful god.

_____ a. Jupiter
_____ b. Neptune
_____ c. Pluto

25. __________________ was not very friendly and the Greek and Roman people feared him.

_____ a. Jupiter
_____ b. Neptune
_____ c. Pluto

PUZZLE OF THE GODS AND GODDESSES

CLUES FOR PUZZLE OF THE GODS AND GODDESSES

Read each sentence and then look at the list of gods and goddesses. Find the name that correctly completes the sentence and then write the name in the correct place in the crossword puzzle.

DOWN

1. ________________ was the king of Hades.
2. ________________ was the queen of the gods and goddesses.
3. ________________ was the goddess of the moon and hunting.
4. The goddess, ______________, was the queen of Hades.
5. ________________ was the god of strength.
6. The goddess, ______________, controlled love and beauty.
7. ________________ was the goddess of the harvest.
8. ________________ was the king of the gods and goddesses.
9. ________________ was the god of wine.
10. ________________ was the goddess of youth.

ACROSS

1. The god, ________________, controlled love.
2. ____________________ controlled the sun.
3. ____________________ was the god of war.
4. ____________________ controlled time.
5. ____________________ was the messenger of the gods and goddesses.
6. ______________ was the goddess of the hearth.
7. The god, ______________, controlled the sea.
8. ________________ controlled fire.
9. ______________ was the goddess of wisdom.

SECTION II

MYTHS ❖ GROUP ONE

GLOSSARY

THE FIRST FROGS

1. angry	mad
2. to croak	to make a noise like a frog
3. to decide (decided)	to make up one's mind
4. frogs	small jumping animals with webbed feet that live in or near water
5. muddy	dirty
6. to pity (pitied)	to feel sorry for
7. pond	a small area of water
8. to rest	to sit or lie down quietly
9. to shake	to move back and forth quickly
10. stones	small rocks
11. to swallow (swallowed)	to allow food to go into the stomach
12. webbed	connected by skin

THE LAUREL TREE

1. arrows	pointed sticks shot from a bow
2. bow	a weapon for shooting arrows
3. to chase	to follow quickly
4. to choose (chose)	to pick one thing from a group
5. favorite	liked better than others
6. frightened	scared or afraid
7. handsome	nice looking
8. laurel	a kind of tree that stays green all year
9. maiden	a young unmarried woman
10. to remember	to think about for a long time
11. tricks	things done to fool someone
12. wreath	a circle made of leaves or branches
13. woods	a forest; many trees growing in one area

SIX POMEGRANATE SEEDS

1. agreement	a decision made by two or more people
2. to arrive (arrived)	to come to a place
3. extremely	very
4. joy	happiness
5. lovely	pretty
6. to order (ordered)	to tell someone what to do
7. pomegranate	a kind of fruit with many seeds inside
8. queen	the wife of a king
9. rule	something to obey; a law
10. seasons	summer, fall, winter, or spring
11. seeds	parts of a plant from which another plant may grow

NARCISSUS

1. depressed	sad
2. to ignore (ignored)	to pay no attention to someone or something
3. mirror	a glass that shows a likeness or copy of someone or something
4. reflection	something seen like in a mirror

PANDORA

1. curious	wanting to know
2. evil	very bad, awful, terrible
3. fairy	a tiny character that can do magic things
4. gift	something given to another person for a special reason
5. healthy	well, free from sickness
6. hunger	the problem of needing food
7. plenty	enough
8. poverty	the problem of being poor
9. special	important
10. to sting (stung)	to hurt with a sharp pointed object

THE FIRST FROGS

Once there was a woman. Her name was Latona. The gods and goddesses were angry at her because she did something bad. They would not let her rest. When she sat down, they would make the earth shake. Even the people did not like Latona. When Latona came near, the people would make her go away.

One day she was very thirsty. She found a pond. She went to the pond to get a drink. Some boys saw Latona. The boys started to throw stones at her. Then the boys threw stones into the water. The boys walked in the water and made it very muddy. The boys were awful.

Latona asked the gods and goddesses for help. They pitied Latona. They decided to help Latona.

The gods and goddesses changed the boys into frogs. The boys became small and fat, green and brown. Their hands and feet were webbed like ducks' feet. The boys could no longer talk. They began to croak. They no longer ate typical food. They swallowed flies and worms.

The Greek and Roman people believed that the boys became the first frogs.

THE FIRST FROGS
STUDY QUESTIONS

Match the words on the left with the meanings on the right. Write a letter from the right in the correct blank on the left.

______1. webbed
______2. pity
______3. pond
______4. croak
______5. shake

a. to make a sound like a frog
b. a small area of water
c. connected by skin
d. to feel sorry for
e. to eat
f. to move back and forth quickly

Look at the words below. Then read each sentence. Write the correct word or words in the blank in each sentence.

muddy **gods and goddesses** **swallowed** **frogs** **earth** **thirsty**

6. The gods and goddesses changed the boys into ______________________________.

7. The boys walked in the pond, and it became ______________________________.

8. The ________________________________ would not let Latona rest.

9. The gods and goddesses made the ________________________ shake when Latona sat down.

10. The boys ________________________ flies and worms.

11. *Read the words below. Circle the characters from the myth.*

Latona **girls** **Apollo** **gods** **goddesses** **boys** **Laurel**

12. *Circle the correct answer.* Latona was a ______________________________.

god **woman** **goddess** **man**

13. *Circle the correct answer.* The boys were ___________________________.

gods **humans** **goddesses** **flies**

14. *Read the sentences below. Write 1, 2, 3, 4, or 5 in each blank to show what happened 1st, 2nd, 3rd, 4th, or 5th.*

______ Some boys were mean to Latona.

______ The gods and goddesses felt sorry for Latona.

______ The gods and goddesses were angry at Latona.

______ The gods and goddesses changed the boys into frogs.

______ Latona went to a pond to get a drink.

Read the sentences and questions below. Write the correct sentence in each blank.

They threw rocks at her.
They swallowed flies.
They changed them into frogs.
They made the earth shake.
They made her go away.

15. What did the gods and goddesses do when Latona sat down? ______________________

____

____

16. What did the boys do to Latona? ______________________

____

____

17. What did many people do when Latona came near? ______________________

____

____

18. What did the gods and goddesses do to the boys? ______________________

____

____

Read the sentence and phrases below. Check each phrase that correctly completes the sentence.

After the boys became frogs, they ______________________.

______ 19. threw rocks into the pond

______ 20. had webbed feet and hands

______ 21. began to croak and did not talk

______ 22. ate flies and worms for food

______ 23. made the earth shake

______ 24. became small and fat, green and brown

Read the phrases and sentences below. Fill in each blank with the correct phrase.

to make the water muddy
because she did something bad
to get a drink
because they were awful
because they could not talk
because they pitied her

25. The gods and goddesses punished Latona ____

____.

26. Latona went to the pond ____

____.

27. The boys walked in the pond ____

____.

28. The gods and goddesses helped Latona ____

____.

29. The gods and goddesses changed the boys into frogs ______________________________

____.

Read the sentence and phrases below. Check each phrase that correctly completes the sentence.

The Greek and Roman people believed ____.

______ 30. that this myth was not a true story

______ 31. that the boys became the first frogs

______ 32. that this myth explained something that they did not understand

______ 33. that the gods and goddesses controlled the boys and Latona

______ 34. that this myth was a true story

______ 35. that this myth explained about emotions

THE LAUREL TREE

Venus was a goddess. She was the goddess of love. She had a son. Her son's name was Cupid. Cupid was the god of love. Cupid had a bow and some arrows. Cupid shot people with the arrows. Some of the arrows caused people to love. Some of the arrows made people hate or become afraid. Cupid liked to play tricks on people and other gods and goddesses.

Apollo was a god. He was the god of the sun. He was young and handsome.

Daphne was a maiden. She lived in the woods. She loved to walk in the woods. She liked her easy life.

One day, Cupid wanted to play a trick on Apollo and Daphne. Cupid shot Apollo with a love arrow. Then he shot Daphne with a hate arrow. When Apollo saw Daphne he fell in love with her. Apollo began to chase Daphne. Daphne saw Apollo. She did not like him. Daphne was afraid and tried to run away.

Daphne became very frightened. She asked the gods and goddesses for help. The gods and goddesses changed Daphne into a laurel tree.

Apollo became very sad. Apollo took a branch from the tree. He made a wreath from the branch. He put the wreath on his head. He wanted to remember Daphne. Apollo chose the laurel tree as his favorite plant. Laurel trees stay green. The leaves do not die.

The Greek and Roman people believed that Daphne became the first laurel tree.

THE LAUREL TREE
STUDY QUESTIONS

Match the words on the left with the meanings on the right. Write a letter from the right in the correct blank on the left.

______ 1. woods	a. a part of a tree
______ 2. wreath	b. a weapon for shooting arrows
______ 3. maiden	c. a part of the body
______ 4. branch	d. a circle made of leaves or branches
______ 5. bow	e. forest
	f. a young woman

Look at the words below. Then read each sentence. Write the correct word in the blank in each sentence.

laurel **goddess** **handsome** **trick** **chase** **arrows**

6. Cupid shot ________________________ at Daphne and Apollo.

7. Venus was the ________________________ of love.

8. Daphne ran away because Apollo began to ________________________ her.

9. Cupid played a ________________________ on Apollo and Daphne.

10. Apollo was a ________________________ young god.

11. *Read the words below. Circle the characters from the myth.*

    Cupid **Apollo** **Laurel** **Ceres** **Venus** **Daphne**

12. *Circle the correct answer.* Cupid and Apollo were ________________________.

    goddesses **gods** **men** **women**

13. *Circle the correct answer.* Daphne was a ____________________.

    woman **goddess** **god** **man**

14. *Read the sentences below. Write 1, 2, 3, 4, or 5 in each blank to show what happened 1st, 2nd, 3rd, 4th, or 5th.*

    ______ Apollo fell in love with Daphne and began to chase her.

    ______ The gods and goddesses changed Daphne into a laurel tree to help her.

    ______ Apollo made a laurel wreath to remember Daphne.

    ______ Cupid shot arrows at Apollo and Daphne.

    ______ Daphne was afraid of Apollo and ran away.

Read the sentences and questions below. Write the correct sentence in each blank.

She ran away from him.
They changed her into a laurel tree.
He shot arrows at them.
He began to chase her.
He made a laurel wreath.

15. What did Apollo do when Daphne became a laurel tree? ______________________________

____

____

16. What did Cupid do to Apollo and Daphne? ______________________________

____

____

17. What did the gods and goddesses do to help Daphne? ______________________________

____

____

18. What did Apollo do when he fell in love with Daphne? ______________________________

____

____

Read the sentence and phrases below. Check each phrase that correctly completes the sentence.

After Daphne became a laurel tree, Apollo ______________________________.

______ 19. took a branch from it

______ 20. wore the wreath to remember Daphne

______ 21. made a laurel bow

______ 22. became very unhappy

______ 23. began to chase her

______ 24. made a laurel wreath

Read the phrases and sentences below. Fill in each blank with the correct phrase.

because she was afraid
to help her
to play a trick on them
because it was green
to make a wreath
because he loved her

25. Apollo began to chase Daphne ______________________________

______________________________.

26. Apollo took a branch from the laurel tree ______________________________

______________________________.

27. Daphne ran away from Apollo ______________________________

______________________________.

28. Cupid shot arrows at Apollo and Daphne ______________________________

______________________________.

29. The gods and goddesses changed Daphne into a laurel tree ______________________________

______________________________.

Read the sentence and phrases below. Check each phrase that correctly completes the sentence.

The Greek and Roman people believed ______________________________.

______ 30. that Cupid was the god who controlled love and hate

______ 31. that this myth was a true story

______ 32. that Apollo was the god who controlled emotions

______ 33. that this myth was not a true story

______ 34. that this myth explained something about emotions and nature

______ 35. that Daphne became the first laurel tree

THE SIX POMEGRANATE SEEDS

Ceres was a goddess. She took care of all of the flowers, trees, and plants. Ceres had a daughter. Her daughter's name was Proserpina.

Pluto was a god. He lived down far inside the earth. The name of the place was Hades. Pluto was king of Hades. Pluto did not have a queen. He wanted very much to have a queen with him.

One day Pluto left Hades. He went to earth. He looked for a queen. He saw Proserpina. He thought that she was lovely. He wanted her to be his queen. He took her down inside the earth. They went to Hades. He ordered Proserpina to become his queen. She was extremely unhappy. She did not like her new home. She did not like the dark. She did not like Pluto. She wanted to go home to see her mother.

Ceres looked for Proserpina. She looked and looked. She did not find Proserpina. Ceres became sad. She did not take care of the plants. All of the plants died. The people on earth did not have any fruit. The people on earth did not have any vegetables. The earth became ugly without all of the beautiful trees and flowers. The people on the earth asked the gods and goddesses to help.

Mercury was a god. He told the people that he would help. He would go to Hades and get Proserpina.

When Mercury arrived in Hades, he learned something important. There was one kind of fruit that grew in Hades. It was called a pomegranate. A pomegranate has many seeds inside of it. Pluto had a rule: ANYONE WHO ATE SOME OF THE POMEGRANATE SEEDS COULD NOT LEAVE HADES. Proserpina did not know about this rule. She ate six of the pomegranate seeds.

Pluto said to Mercury, "Proserpina ate six of the pomegranate seeds. She cannot leave Hades. She must stay with me forever."

Mercury said to Pluto, "The people on earth need plants. Ceres will not take care of the plants. She is sad because her daughter is gone."

Mercury and Pluto made an agreement. Proserpina must stay with Pluto for six months because she ate six seeds. Then Proserpina could stay with her mother for six months.

When Proserpina went home, her mother was very happy. Her mother took care of the plants. The plants grew. The earth was pretty again. The earth was full of joy.

When Proserpina would go back to Pluto's home, Ceres would not take care of the plants. The plants would die. The earth would be quiet and ugly.

The Greek and Roman people believed that this myth explained about the four seasons. They thought that fall and winter happened when Proserpina lived with Pluto. They thought that was the time when Ceres was sad and did not take care of the plants. The Greeks and Romans also thought that spring and summer happened when Proserpina lived with Ceres. They thought that was the time when Ceres was happy and took care of the plants.

THE SIX POMEGRANATE SEEDS
STUDY QUESTIONS

Match the words on the left with the meanings on the right. Write a letter from the right in the correct blank on the left.

______ 1. seasons	a. a kind of fruit that has many seeds inside of it
______ 2. queen	b. a decision made by two or more people
______ 3. agreement	c. a place where people live
______ 4. pomegranate	d. the wife of a king
______ 5. rule	e. something to obey; a law
	f. summer, fall, winter, spring

Look at the words below. Then read each sentence. Write the correct word in the blank in each sentence.

earth **plants** **quiet** **seeds** **months** **Hades**

6. Proserpina lived on the earth for six ____________________________.

7. All of the____ died when Ceres was unhappy.

8. A pomegranate has many __________________________ inside of it.

9. Pluto wanted a queen to live with him in ______________________________ .

10. The __________________________ was beautiful when the trees and flowers grew.

11. *Read the words below. Circle the characters from the myth.*

Hades **Earth** **Ceres** **Mercury** **Proserpina** **Pluto**

12. *Circle the correct answer.* Pluto and Mercury were ________________________.

women **gods** **men** **goddesses**

13. *Circle the correct answer.* Ceres and Proserpina were ________________________.

women **gods** **men** **goddesses**

14. *Read the sentences below. Write 1, 2, 3, 4, or 5 in each blank to show what happened 1st, 2nd, 3rd, 4th, or 5th.*

______ Mercury helped the people by talking to Pluto about Proserpina.

______ Mercury and Pluto made an agreement.

______ Pluto took Proserpina to Hades to be his queen.

______ Proserpina lived on earth for six months and in Hades for six months.

______ Ceres did not take care of the plants and the people on earth were unhappy.

Read the sentences and questions below. Write the correct sentence in each blank.

He made an agreement with Pluto.
He looked for a queen.
She ate six pomegranate seeds.
She took care of the plants.
She let the plants die.

15. What did Pluto do when he went to earth? ______________________________

____

____

16. What did Proserpina do when she was in Hades? ______________________________

____

____

17. What did Mercury do when he went to Hades? ______________________________

____

____

18. What did Ceres do when Proserpina lived on earth?______________________________

____

____

Read the sentence and phrases below. Check each phrase that correctly completes the sentence.

After Pluto and Mercury made the agreement, ______________________________.

______ 19. Ceres took care of the plants for six months

______ 20. Mercury would live in Hades for six months

______ 21. Pluto could keep his queen for six months

______ 22. the pomegranate would grow on earth for six months

______ 23. the earth would be ugly for six months

______ 24. Proserpina could leave Hades for six months

Read the phrases and sentences below. Fill in each blank with the correct phrase.

because she ate six pomegranate seeds
because she was hungry
to talk with Pluto
because she was sad
to be his queen
because Ceres took care of the plants

25. Ceres did not take care of the plants ______________________________

____.

26. The earth was beautiful ______________________________

____.

27. Pluto took Proserpina to Hades ______________________________

____.

28. At first, Pluto said that Proserpina could not leave Hades ______________________________

____.

29. Mercury went to Hades ______________________________

____.

Read the sentence and phrases below. Check each phrase that correctly completes the sentence.

The Greek and Roman people believed ______________________________.

______ 30. that this myth was a true story

______ 31. that this myth explained the six seasons

______ 32. that this myth was not a true story

______ 33. that this myth explained something about nature that they did not understand

______ 34. that the gods and goddesses never helped the people on earth

______ 35. that this myth explained about summer, fall, winter, and spring

NARCISSUS

Once there was a boy named Narcissus. He was very handsome. He did not know that he was handsome. He could not see his face because he did not have a mirror.

Many maidens fell in love with Narcissus. They thought he was handsome. They wanted to be with him. When the maidens came near him, he ignored them.

One day, Narcissus went to a pond to get a drink. He sat by the pond. When he started to drink he saw his face in the pond. He did not know that the face was his own reflection. He loved the face that he saw in the pond. He wanted the face to love him. The face could not love him because it was not real. It was his own reflection.

Narcissus did not want to leave the pond. He sat by the pond many days and many nights. He did not eat. He became very depressed. After a while, he died.

The gods and goddesses changed Narcissus into a beautiful flower. They named the flower narcissus.

The Greek and Roman people believed that the boy became the first narcissus. The name of the flower was copied from the boy's name.

NARCISSUS
STUDY QUESTIONS

Match the words on the left with the meanings on the right. Write a letter from the right in the correct blank on the left.

______ 1. pond	a. a young woman
______ 2. reflection	b. sad
______ 3. flower	c. something seen like in a mirror
______ 4. depressed	d. a small area of water
______ 5. maiden	e. to buy some flowers
	f. a part of a plant

Look at the words below. Then read each sentence. Write the correct word in the blank in each sentence.

gods **mirror** **ignored** **handsome** **drink** **flower**

6. Narcissus wanted to get a ____________________ at the pond.
7. Narcissus did not know he was handsome because he did not have a ____________________.
8. Narcissus ____________________ the maidens when they came near him.
9. The gods and goddesses changed the boy into a ____________________.
10. The maidens thought Narcissus was ____________________.
11. *Read the words below. Circle the characters from the myth.*

    Narcissus **Pluto** **Neptune** **maidens** **pond** **Pandora**

12. *Circle the correct answer.* Narcissus was a ____________________ .

    girl **god** **boy** **goddess**

13. *Circle the correct answer.* The maidens were ____________________.

    girls **gods** **boys** **goddesses**

14. *Read the sentences below. Write 1, 2, 3, 4, or 5 in each blank to show what happened 1st, 2nd, 3rd, 4th, or 5th.*

    ______ Narcissus went to a pond and saw his reflection.

    ______ He did not eat and became depressed.

    ______ Narcissus died and the gods and goddesses changed him into a flower.

    ______ The maidens wanted to be with Narcissus, but he ignored them.

    ______ He fell in love with his own face and did not want to leave the pond.

Read the sentences and questions below. Write the correct sentence in each blank.

They ignored him.
He saw his reflection.
He ignored them.
They changed him into a flower.
He loved it.

15. What did the gods and goddesses do to Narcissus? ____________________

____

____

16. What did Narcissus do when the maidens came near him? ____________________

____

____

17. What did Narcissus do at the pond? ____________________

____

____

18. What did Narcissus do when he saw his reflection? ____________________

____

____

Read the sentence and phrases below. Check each phrase that correctly completes the sentence.

After Narcissus saw his reflection, he____________________.

______ 19. wanted the face to love him

______ 20. loved the maidens

______ 21. did not leave the pond

______ 22. did not eat

______ 23. ignored it

______ 24. became depressed

Read the phrases and sentences below. Fill in each blank with the correct phrase.

because he did not eat and became depressed
to get a drink
because he did not have a mirror
because it was not real
to change him into a flower
because they loved him

25. The maidens wanted to be near Narcissus ______________________________

______________________________.

26. At first, Narcissus did not see his face ______________________________

______________________________.

27. The reflection could not love Narcissus ______________________________

______________________________.

28. Narcissus died ______________________________

______________________________.

29. Narcissus went to the pond ______________________________

______________________________.

Read the sentence and phrases below. Check each phrase that correctly completes the sentence.

The Greek and Roman people believed ______________________________.

______ 30. that this myth explained something about nature

______ 31. that the gods and goddesses never helped the people on earth

______ 32. that the boy became the first narcissus

______ 33. that the boy became the first maiden

______ 34. that this myth was a true story

______ 35. that this myth was not a true story

PANDORA

A long time ago, the world was a wonderful place. The people were always healthy. They were always happy and loved each other. They had plenty of food and money.

A young woman lived on earth. Her name was Pandora. The gods and goddesses thought she was beautiful. They gave her many gifts. One day the gods and goddesses sent Mercury to see her. He brought her a special gift. It was a beautiful box. Mercury told Pandora, "The gods and goddesses want you to keep this box and never open it."

Pandora was a very curious young girl. She wanted to open the box. She wanted to see inside it. After a while, she opened the box. Many terrible things flew out of the box. They all looked different, but they were all very ugly. The names of some of these bad things were Sickness, Poverty, Anger, Hate, and Hunger. The evil things stung Pandora. They hurt her and then she cried. Pandora became sick.

The terrible things flew out of her home. They stung many people on earth. Some of the people became sick. Some of the people became unhappy. Some of the people began to hate each other. Some of the people became hungry. Some of the people became poor.

Pandora was sad. After a while, Pandora heard a sound in the box. She opened the box again and a pretty little fairy flew out. The fairy's name was Hope. Hope kissed Pandora and made her feel better. Hope flew away. Hope kissed many of the people. Many people felt better. When people have problems, they feel bad. They want Hope to come and help them. They want Hope to make them feel better so they will be happy.

The Greek and Roman people believed that poverty, sickness, hate, and many other bad things began on earth when Pandora opened the box. They also believed that hope was a good thing that began on earth when Pandora opened the box.

PANDORA
STUDY QUESTIONS

Match the words on the left with the meanings on the right. Write a letter from the right in the correct blank on the left.

______ 1. evil	a. the problem of being ill
______ 2. sound	b. the problem of needing food
______ 3. poverty	c. bad; awful; terrible
______ 4. curious	d. noise
______ 5. hunger	e. wanting to know
	f. the problem of being poor

Look at the words below. Then read each sentence. Write the correct word in the blank in each sentence.

problems **fairy** **healthy** **hope** **gift** **box**

6. A good feeling that came from the box is called ______________________________.

7. The people were ______________________________ before Pandora opened the box.

8. The gods and goddesses gave Pandora a box as a ______________________________.

9. Hope was the name of a good ______________________________.

10. Some ______________________________ that people have are poverty and sickness.

11. *Read the words below. Circle the characters from the myth.*

Pluto **Pandora** **Apollo** **Proserpina** **Mercury** **Narcissus**

12. *Circle the correct answer.* Pandora was a ___________________________.

woman **god** **man** **goddess**

13. *Circle the correct answer.* Mercury was a ________________________.

woman **god** **man** **goddess**

14. *Read the sentences below. Write 1, 2, 3, 4, or 5 in each blank to show what happened 1st, 2nd, 3rd, 4th, or 5th.*

______ Pandora was curious and opened the box.

______ Then Pandora found Hope and many people felt better.

______ The gods and goddesses gave Pandora a box and told her never to open it.

______ Pandora and the people were unhappy.

______ Many evil things flew out of her home and stung people on earth.

Read the sentences and questions below. Write the correct sentence in each blank.

She kissed them and made them feel better.
She opened it.
He gave it to Pandora.
They stung them.
They helped them feel better.

15. What did Pandora do to the box? ____

____

____

16. What did Hope do to the people? ____

____

____

17. What did the evil things do to the people? ______________________________

____

____

18. What did Mercury do with the box? ______________________________________

____

____

Read the sentence and phrases below. Check each phrase that correctly completes the sentence.

After Pandora opened the box, ____.

______ 19. all of the people on earth were healthy and happy

______ 20. poverty, sickness, and many bad things were finished on earth

______ 21. Hope never helped the people feel better

______ 22. some of the terrible things stung many people

______ 23. people learned that hope was a good thing

______ 24. hunger, hate, and many problems began on earth

Read the phrases and sentences below. Fill in each blank with the correct phrase.

because they did not have any problems on earth
to make them feel better
to give a box to Pandora
because the evil things hurt her
because she was curious

25. Pandora opened the box ______________________________

______________________________.

26. Hope kissed many people ______________________________

______________________________.

27. Pandora cried and became sick ______________________________

______________________________.

28. At first, the people were always happy ______________________________

______________________________.

29. Mercury went to earth ______________________________

______________________________.

Read the sentence and phrases below. Check each phrase that correctly completes the sentence.

The Greek and Roman people believed ______________________________.

______ 30. that this myth explained how bad things began on earth

______ 31. that this myth explained how hope helps people feel better

______ 32. that this myth was a true story

______ 33. that this myth explains something they did not understand

______ 34. that the people on earth will always be happy

______ 35. that this myth was not a true story

EVALUATION
For Section II

PART I - CHARACTERS

Match the names on the left with the phrases on the right. Write the letter of the correct phrase in each blank on the left.

____ 1. Pluto
____ 2. Hope
____ 3. Apollo
____ 4. Cupid
____ 5. Ceres
____ 6. Proserpina
____ 7. Latona
____ 8. Mercury
____ 9. Narcissus
____10. Daphne
____11. Venus
____12. Pandora

a. a maiden who became a tree
b. a woman who became a frog
c. a fairy who made some people feel better
d. a handsome boy who became a flower
e. a woman who made the gods and goddesses angry
f. a young woman who was very curious
g. the god of the sun
h. the goddess who takes care of plants
i. the goddess of love
j. the queen of Hades
k. the messenger of the gods and goddesses
l. the god of love
m. the king of Hades

PART II - NOUNS

Write the correct word for each meaning.

maiden hunger pond seasons pomegranate wreath earth
agreement seeds fairy king frogs branch arrows stones bow

13. ______________: small rocks

14. ______________: a small area of water

15. ______________: a kind of fruit that has many seeds inside

16. ______________: the problem of needing food

17. ______________: a circle of leaves or branches

18. ______________: summer, fall, winter, spring

19. ______________: a male who controls a place

20. ______________: a young unmarried woman

21. ______________: a weapon for shooting arrows

22. ______________: the land on which people live

23. ______________: a decision made by two people

24. ______________: a part of a tree

25. ______________: pointed sticks which are shot from a bow

26. ______________: the parts of a plant from which another plant grows

27. ______________: small animals with webbed feet

PART III - VERBS

Read each sentence. Fill in each blank with the letter of the correct answer.

28. The word *stung* means_________________.

    a. hit with a stick
    b. hurt with a sharp pointed object
    c. hunted with a gun

29. The word *copied* means_________________.

    a. made differently
    b. made new
    c. made the same

30. The word *ignored* means_________________.

    a. not paid
    b. paid attention
    c. paid no attention

31. The word *loved* means_________________.

    a. thought about
    b. liked very much
    c. wrote often

32. The word *ordered* means_________________.

    a. told what to do
    b. bought from a store
    c. asked about a friend

33. The word *rest* means_________________.

    a. fight with friends
    b. grabbed by the police
    c. sit or lie down quietly

34. The word *croak* means_________________.

    a. to make a soft noise
    b. to make a noise like a cow
    c. to make a noise like a frog

35. The word *chase* means_________________.

    a. grab one time
    b. follow quickly
    c. tie up

36. The word *remember* means_________________.

    a. to think about for a long time
    b. to look at for a long time
    c. to want for a long time

37. The word *flew* means_________________.

    a. moved through the water with feet
    b. moved through the water with hands
    c. moved through the air with wings

38. The word *heard* means_________________.

    a. wanted
    b. told about
    c. listened

39. The word *pitied* means_________________.

    a. felt sorry for
    b. felt sad about
    c. felt angry at

40. The word *shake* means_________________.

    a. to go under and over
    b. to move back and forth
    c. to sit beside and behind

PART IV - ADJECTIVES

Look at the words below. Then read each sentence. Write the correct word in the blank in each sentence.

angry thirsty depressed frightened favorite healthy webbed
easy quiet beautiful fat six muddy handsome special terrible

41. Narcissus became ______________________ because the face in the water did not love him.

42. Proserpina ate ______________________ pomegranate seeds.

43. Apollo was a young and ______________________ god.

44. When the boys became frogs, they had ______________________ feet and hands.

45. When Pandora opened the box, ______________________ things flew out.

46. Earth was very ugly and ______________________ when Ceres did not take care of the plants.

47. The gods and goddesses were ______________________ at Latona because she did something bad.

48. When the boys walked in the water, it became ______________________.

49. Apollo chose the laurel tree as his ______________________ plant.

50. The gods and goddesses gave Pandora a ______________________ gift.

51. Daphne became ______________________ when Apollo began to chase her.

52. Long ago the world was wonderful and the people on earth were______________________ .

53. Narcissus was changed into a ______________________ flower.

54. Latona went to the pond because she was ______________________.

55. When the boys changed into frogs, they became ______________________ and small.

PART V - SEQUENCE

Read the sentences below. Write 1, 2, 3, or 4 in each blank to show what happened 1st, 2nd, 3rd, and 4th.

THE FIRST FROGS

56. ______ The gods and goddesses pitied Latona and wanted to help her.
______ Latona went to the pond because she was thirsty.
______ The gods and goddesses changed the boys into frogs.
______ Some boys were awful and threw rocks at her.

THE LAUREL TREE

57. ______ Apollo chose the laurel tree as his favorite plant.
______ Apollo fell in love with Daphne and she became frightened.
______ The gods and goddesses helped Daphne by changing her into a laurel tree.
______ Cupid shot arrows at Apollo and Daphne.

THE SIX POMEGRANATE SEEDS

58. ______ Ceres was sad and did not take care of the plants on earth.
______ Mercury and Pluto made an agreement about Proserpina.
______ Proserpina lived with Ceres for six months and with Pluto for six months.
______ Pluto took Proserpina to Hades to be his queen.

NARCISSUS

59. ______ Narcissus fell in love with his own face.
______ The gods and goddesses changed Narcissus into a flower.
______ Narcissus went to the pond and saw his reflection.
______ Narcissus was sad because the face did not love him.

PANDORA

60. ______ A fairy named Hope kissed people and made them feel better.
______ Pandora was curious and opened the box.
______ Many terrible things flew out of the box and made many people unhappy.
______ The gods and goddesses gave Pandora a box and told her not to open it.

PART VI - GREEK AND ROMAN BELIEFS

Read the sentence and phrases below. Check each phrase that correctly completes the sentence.

The Greek and Roman people believed ____.

______ 61. that myths were not true

______ 62. that Narcissus became a flower

______ 63. that sometimes the gods and goddesses helped people on earth

______ 64. that some bad things happened on earth when Pandora became curious

______ 65. that Mercury controlled the four seasons

______ 66. that Latona became the first frog

______ 67. that some myths explained about emotions and nature

______ 68. that Hope was the god of poverty and hate

______ 69. that some myths explained things they did not understand

______ 70. that Apollo planted the first laurel tree

SECTION III

MYTHS ❖ GROUP TWO

GLOSSARY

DAEDALUS AND ICARUS

1. to drown (drowned)	to die under water
2. to escape	to go away without permission
3. famous	known by many people
4. feathers	things that cover a bird's body
5. idea	an important thought
6. inventor	a person who thinks of a new idea
7. island	an area of land with water around it
8. to melt (melted)	to become soft
9. to obey	to do what someone tells you to do
10. tower	a tall building
11. wings	the parts of a bird's body used in flying

PROMETHEUS AND THE FIRE

1. to chain (chained)	to hold together
2. chains	metal circles that are joined together
3. claws	sharp parts of an animal's body
4. fur	something that covers an animal's body
5. giants	large, strong humanlike characters
6. to hurry (hurried)	to go quickly
7. to peck	to hurt with a bird's beak
8. permission	allowing someone to do something
9. to protect	to keep something away from danger
10. to punish (punished)	to cause someone pain for doing something wrong
11. raw	not cooked
12. to steal (stole)	to take without permission
13. to suffer	to feel pain or sadness
14. torch	a stick with fire at one end

HYACINTHUS

1. to bloom (bloomed)	to open into a flower
2. butterflies	flying insects
3. dearly	very much; fondly
4. flower bed	a part of a garden that has flowers
5. horseshoe	the iron shoe of a horse used to play the game of horseshoes
6. horseshoes	the name of a game; throwing a horse's shoes at an iron stake
7. jealous	wanting something or someone who belongs to another
8. meadow	a grassy field

IRIS

1. bridge	something that joins two places together
2. to cross (crossed)	to go over
3. end	the place where something stops
4. indigo	a dark purple color
5. meeting	a time when a group of people talk about a plan
6. messages	words sent to someone
7. to permit (permitted)	to let someone do something
8. rainbow	something curved that appears in the sky and has seven colors
9. to suggest (suggested)	to tell an idea
10. violet	a light purple color
11. to visit	to go see

AURORA AND TITHONUS

1. to beg (begged)	to ask for something
2. charming	very kind or very nice
3. dawn	early morning
4. forever	always; never stopping
5. to hop	to jump
6. pale	light in color
7. voice	sound made when someone talks
8. wise	smart
9. wrinkled	folded skin

DAEDALUS AND ICARUS

Daedalus was a famous inventor. He made many things for King Minos. One day the king became angry at Daedalus. The king put Daedalus in a tower on an island.

Daedalus had a son. His son's name was Icarus. Icarus helped his father escape from the tower. Daedalus and Icarus wanted to escape from the island. They wanted to go home. Daedalus had an idea. He wanted to fly away from the island. He made some wings. He used wax and feathers. Soon Daedalus finished the wings. Daedalus and Icarus tied the wings to their arms.

Daedalus told Icarus, "Do not fly close to the sun. The sun is hot. The sun will melt the wax. Then the feathers will fall from your arms."

Icarus was a young man. Icarus ignored what his father said. Icarus did not listen. He flew near the sun. The wax melted and the feathers fell off. Icarus fell into the sea and drowned. Daedalus was very sad.

The Greek and Roman people believed that this myth taught them a lesson. They learned to obey their parents. They learned to obey people who knew many things. Sometimes, when people do not obey, bad things may happen to them.

DAEDALUS AND ICARUS
STUDY QUESTIONS

Match the words on the left with the meanings on the right. Write a letter from the right in the correct blank on the left.

______ 1. island	a. to die under the water
______ 2. inventor	b. an area of land with water around it
______ 3. wings	c. parts of a person's body
______ 4. drown	d. a tall building
______ 5. tower	e. a person who thinks of a new idea
	f. the parts of a bird's body used in flying

Look at the words below. Then read each sentence. Write the correct word in the blank in each sentence.

ignored **feathers** **colors** **escape** **melted** **wax** **arms**

6. The ____________________ melted because the sun was hot.

7. Daedalus made wings and tied them to his ______________________.

8. Icarus ________________ what Daedalus told him.

9. The wax melted and the _______________________ fell off.

10. Daedalus and Icarus wanted to ______________________ from the island.

11. *Read the words below. Circle the characters from the myth.*

Daphne **island** **Icarus** **King Minos** **Daedalus** **feathers**

12. *Circle the correct answer.* Icarus was the ___________________ of Daedalus.

Inventor **son** **daughter** **god**

13. *Circle the correct answer.* Daedalus was an ____________________.

son **inventor** **daughter** **god**

14. *Read the sentences below. Write 1, 2, 3, 4, or 5 in each blank to show what happened 1st, 2nd, 3rd, 4th, or 5th.*

______ Icarus ignored his father and flew near the sun.

______ Daedalus and Icarus tied wings to their arms.

______ The feathers fell off of Icarus and he drowned in the sea.

______ Daedalus made wings.

______ Daedalus told Icarus about the hot sun.

Read the sentences and questions below. Write the correct sentence in each blank.

He made wings.
He put him in a tower on an island.
He fell into the sea.
They tied them to their arms.
He made many things.

15. What did Daedalus and Icarus do with the wings? ______________________________

____

____

16. What did Daedalus do for King Minos? ______________________________________

____

____

17. What did Daedalus do with the wax and feathers? ____________________________

____

____

18. What did King Minos do to Daedalus? ______________________________________

____

____

Read the sentence and phrases below. Check each phrase that correctly completes the sentence.

After Icarus flew near the sun, ____.

_____ 19. the feathers fell from his arms

_____ 20. he learned to obey his father

_____ 21. he drowned in the sea

_____ 22. the wax melted

_____ 23. Daedalus was very happy

_____ 24. he went back to the tower

Read the phrases and sentences below. Fill in each blank with the correct phrase.

to escape from the island
because Icarus flew near the sun
because he ignored his father
because he fell into the sea
because he was angry
to make wings

25. Daedalus used feathers and wax ______________________________

______________________________.

26. The wax melted ______________________________

______________________________.

27. Daedalus made wings ______________________________

______________________________.

28. King Minos put Daedalus in a tower ______________________________

______________________________.

29. Icarus flew near the sun ______________________________

______________________________.

Read the sentence and phrases below. Check each phrase that correctly completes the sentence.

The Greek and Roman people believed ______________________________.

______ 30. that this myth taught people to obey their parents

______ 31. that this myth was not a true story

______ 32. that this myth was a true story

______ 33. that Icarus and Daedalus became the first birds

______ 34. that the gods and goddesses helped Daedalus and Icarus

______ 35. that sometimes bad things happen when people do not obey

PROMETHEUS AND THE FIRE

Jupiter was the king of the gods and goddesses. He sent two Titans, Prometheus and his brother Epimetheus, to the earth. The Titans were a group of strong Greek giants. Epimetheus made all of the animals on the earth. Prometheus made all of the men and women on the earth.

The animals could protect themselves. They could find food easily. The animals had warm fur, sharp claws, and strong legs. The people could not protect themselves. They were cold. They ate raw food. They did not know how to make fire, to keep warm, or to cook their food. They were unhappy.

Prometheus pitied the people. He wanted to help them. He did not want the people to suffer. One day Prometheus went to Mount Olympus. The other gods and goddesses did not see him. He lit a torch with fire from the sun. Prometheus hurried back to earth with the fire.

Prometheus showed his friends on earth how to use the fire. They built fires to keep warm. They learned to cook their food. Fire frightened wild animals away. The people on earth were happy with the fire. They thanked Prometheus. They thought fire was a wonderful gift.

Jupiter was angry because Prometheus stole the fire from the sun. Jupiter said, "Only gods and goddesses can use fire! You did not ask permission to get the fire from the sun. I will punish you."

Jupiter punished Prometheus. He chained Prometheus to a rock. Then Jupiter sent birds to peck at Prometheus's body. For many years, Prometheus stayed on the rock. He was very lonely. He thought that he would never be free again.

One day, a very strong man came to Prometheus. His name was Hercules. Hercules broke the chains. Prometheus was free. Prometheus thanked Hercules. Prometheus said, "I will help you someday, too."

The Greek and Roman people believed that this myth explained about fire. They thought that Prometheus brought the first fire to earth from the sun.

PROMETHEUS AND THE FIRE
STUDY QUESTIONS

Match the words on the left with the meanings on the right. Write a letter from the right in the correct blank on the left.

______ 1. torch	a. heat and light made by something burning
______ 2. peck	b. a stick with fire at one end
______ 3. giants	c. large, strong humanlike characters
______ 4. fire	d. to keep away danger
______ 5. protect	e. to hit with a bird's beak
	f. to swallow quickly

Look at the words below. Then read each sentence. Write the correct word in the blank in each sentence.

chains **suffer** **fur** **rock** **permission** **claws**

6. Prometheus did not ask ______________________ to get the fire.

7. Hercules broke the chains and Prometheus was free from the ________________________.

8. Prometheus did not want the people to ____________________ because they did not have fire.

9. Jupiter put _____________________ on Prometheus.

10. The animals were warm because they had _________________________.

11. *Read the words below. Circle the characters from the myth.*

    Prometheus **Jupiter** **Apollo** **Hercules** **Icarus** **Epimetheus**

12. *Circle the correct answer.* Prometheus and Epimetheus were___________________.

    giants **animals** **goddesses** **birds**

13. *Circle the correct answer.* Jupiter was a ________________________.

    giant **bird** **goddess** **god**

14. *Read the sentences below. Write 1, 2, 3, 4, or 5 in each blank to show what happened 1st, 2nd, 3rd, 4th, or 5th.*

    ______ Prometheus went to Mount Olympus and stole fire from the sun.

    ______ The people on earth did not know how to make fire.

    ______ Finally, Hercules broke the chains and Prometheus was free.

    ______ Jupiter was angry and chained Prometheus to a rock.

    ______ Prometheus wanted to help the people on earth.

Read the sentences and questions below. Write the correct sentence in each blank.

They came to peck at his body.
They were cold and ate raw food.
He broke the chains.
He lit a torch with fire from the sun.
He punished him.

15. What did Prometheus do on Mount Olympus? ______________________________

____

____

16. What did Jupiter do to Prometheus? ______________________________

____

____

17. What did the birds do to Prometheus? ______________________________

____

____

18. What did Hercules do to help Prometheus? ______________________________

____

____

Read the sentence and phrases below. Check each phrase that correctly completes the sentence.

After Prometheus stole the fire, ____.

_____ 19. the people on earth were happy

_____ 20. Prometheus was chained to a rock for many years

_____ 21. the people on earth could not protect themselves

_____ 22. Jupiter became angry

_____ 23. the people could frighten away the wild animals

_____ 24. the gods and goddesses on Mount Olympus liked him

Read the phrases and sentences below. Fill in each blank with the correct phrase.

to break the chains
to peck at his body
because they thought fire was a wonderful gift
to get fire
because he stole fire from the sun
to help people on earth

25. Prometheus took the fire ____

____.

26. Jupiter sent birds to Prometheus ____

____.

27. The people on earth thanked Prometheus ____

____.

28. Jupiter punished Prometheus ____

____.

29. Prometheus wanted to help people on earth when he went to Mount Olympus ______________

____.

Read the sentence and phrases below. Check each phrase that correctly completes the sentence.

The Greek and Roman people believed ____.

______ 30. that this myth explained about fire

______ 31. that this myth was a true story

______ 32. that the people were happy without fire

______ 33. that this myth was not a true story

______ 34. that this myth explained something they did not understand

______ 35. that Prometheus brought the first fire to the earth

HYACINTHUS

Apollo was the god of the sun. He knew a young boy on earth. His name was Hyacinthus. Apollo and Hyacinthus were friends. Apollo liked Hyacinthus very much. They often played games together.

One spring day, Hyacinthus and Apollo went to a meadow to play a game of horseshoes. It was a beautiful, warm day. The flowers bloomed and the birds sang. Lovely butterflies flew all around. Apollo and Hyacinthus felt good. They were very happy. They liked to play horseshoes together.

Zephyrus was the name of the wind. Sometimes he was nice. Many times he was mean. Zephyrus saw Apollo and Hyacinthus playing horseshoes together. Zephyrus was jealous. He knew that Apollo liked Hyacinthus.

One time Apollo threw a horseshoe. Zephyrus was a strong wind. He blew the horseshoe back to Hyacinthus. The horseshoe hit Hyacinthus in the head. Hyacinthus fell into a flower bed and died. Apollo said, "I will never forget you, Hyacinthus. You were my best friend. I loved you dearly. A new plant will grow where you died. People will look at the plant and will remember you forever."

The next day, people came to the meadow. They saw a beautiful new plant. They named it hyacinth. The plant name was copied from the name of the boy.

The Greeks and Romans believed that this myth explained about the first hyacinth. Many people still enjoy hyacinths in the springtime. A hyacinth has many flowers. The flowers look like small bells. Hyacinths bloom in many different colors. Some of the colors are blue, pink, purple, white, and yellow. Hyacinths most often bloom in March or April.

HYACINTHUS
STUDY QUESTIONS

Match the words on the left with the meanings on the right. Write a letter from the right in the correct blank on the left.

______ 1. horseshoes	a. a grassy field
______ 2. hyacinth	b. a game
______ 3. flower bed	c. a part of a garden
______ 4. butterflies	d. to bloom
______ 5. meadow	e. flying insects
	f. a kind of flower

Look at the words below. Then read each sentence. Write the correct word in the blank in each sentence.

jealous **horseshoe** **plant** **games** **friend** **bloomed**

6. A ________________________ grew where Hyacinthus died.

7. Zephyrus blew a ________________________ and it hit Hyacinthus.

8. Zephyrus became ________________________ of Apollo and Hyacinthus.

9. Many flowers ________________________ in the meadow.

10. Hyacinthus was Apollo's ________________________.

11. *Read the words below. Circle the characters from the myth.*

Hyacinthus **Apollo** **Horseshoe** **Jupiter** **Iris** **Zephyrus**

12. *Circle the correct answer.* Hyacinthus was a ________________________.

god **girl** **goddess** **boy**

13. *Circle the correct answer.* Apollo was a ________________________.

god **woman** **goddess** **boy**

14. *Read the sentences below. Write 1, 2, 3, 4, or 5 in each blank to show what happened 1st, 2nd, 3rd, 4th, or 5th.*

______ Zephyrus was jealous and blew a horseshoe at Hyacinthus.

______ Some people saw the plant and named it hyacinth.

______ Hyacinthus died and Apollo was sad.

______ A new plant grew where Hyacinthus died.

______ Hyacinthus and Apollo played horseshoes.

Read the sentences and questions below. Write the correct sentence in each blank.

He fell into a flower bed and died.
He blew a horseshoe at Hyacinthus.
They played horseshoes.
He became sad and wept.
They named it.

15. What did Apollo and Hyacinthus often do together? ______________________________

____

____

16. What did the people do when they saw the new plant? ______________________________

____

____

17. What did Zephyrus do when he became jealous? ______________________________

____

____

18. What did Hyacinthus do when the horseshoe hit him? ______________________________

____

____

Read the sentence and phrases below. Check each phrase that correctly completes the sentence.

After Hyacinthus died ____.

______ 19. he fell into bed and went to sleep

______ 20. Apollo wept and thought about his friend

______ 21. Zephyrus blew a horseshoe at him

______ 22. Apollo was happy and forgot his friend

______ 23. some people saw the new plant and thought of him

______ 24. a new plant grew

Read the phrases and sentences below. Fill in each blank with the correct phrase.

because Apollo and Hyacinthus played together
because his friend died
to see a beautiful spring day
because the horseshoe hit his head
to remember Hyacinthus
because he was jealous

25. Zephyrus was jealous ____

____.

26. Hyacinthus died ____

____.

27. Zephyrus blew the horseshoe back to Hyacinthus ______________________

____.

28. Some people named the new plant hyacinth ______________________

____.

29. Apollo wept ____

____.

Read the sentence and phrases below. Check each phrase that correctly completes the sentence.

The Greek and Roman people believed ______________________________.

______ 30. that this myth explained something about nature

______ 31. that this myth was a true story

______ 32. that this myth explained something that they did not understand

______ 33. that the gods and goddesses controlled all games on earth

______ 34. that the name hyacinth was copied from the name of a boy

______ 35. that this myth was not a true story

IRIS

Apollo was the god of the sun. He had a daughter named Iris. Apollo loved Iris very much. He permitted Iris to take messages from him to other gods and goddesses. She often went down to the sea and talked with Neptune. Neptune was the god who controlled the sea. Neptune loved Iris, too. He enjoyed talking to her.

The god of the air and the god of the rain loved Iris, too. They enjoyed talking with her. Soon, the god of the air, the god of the sun, the god of the rain, and the god of the sea decided to have a meeting. They talked about Iris. They wanted Iris to visit the sea, the sky, and the earth often. They planned to build a bridge for Iris. It would be a large and beautiful bridge. It would start in the sky and end on earth.

The four gods wanted the bridge to have beautiful colors. The god of the air wanted the bridge to be the same colors as some flowers. He suggested the colors red, orange, yellow, and green. The god of the sea wanted the bridge to be the same colors as the ocean. He suggested the colors blue and violet. The god of the rain wanted the bridge to have his favorite color on it. He suggested the color indigo.

All of the gods and goddesses met together. They asked the god of the sun to make the bridge. The god of the sun took all of the colors to make the bridge. He used red, orange, yellow, green, blue, indigo, and violet. He made a beautiful bridge. He tied one end of the bridge in the sky. He tied the other end of the bridge on earth.

Iris loved the beautiful bridge. She often crossed the beautiful bridge to visit her favorite gods and goddesses. The colors were always more beautiful when the sun was shining.

The Greek and Roman people believed that this myth explained how rainbows began. A rainbow has seven colors in it. The colors are red, orange, yellow, green, blue, indigo, and violet. A rainbow often appears in the sky after a rainstorm. When the sun shines, the colors become more beautiful.

IRIS
STUDY QUESTIONS

Match the words on the left with the meanings on the right. Write a letter from the right in the correct blank on the left.

______ 1. bridge	a. to go over
______ 2. messages	b. to make
______ 3. favorite	c. a large area of water
______ 4. cross	d. liked very much
______ 5. build	e. words sent to someone
	f. something that joins two places together

Look at the words below. Then read each sentence. Write the correct word in the blank in each sentence.

ocean **rainbow** **colors** **visit** **meeting** **end**

6. The Greeks and Romans believed the bridge was the first ______________________.

7. The bridge had seven ______________________.

8. One ______________________ of the bridge was on earth and the other in the sky.

9. Iris liked to ______________________ her favorite gods and goddesses.

10. Four gods had a ______________________ to talk about Iris.

11. *Read the words below. Circle the characters from the myth.*

    Apollo **Neptune** **Indigo** **Iris** **Icarus** **Jupiter**

12. *Circle the correct answer.* Neptune and Apollo were ______________________.

    gods **goddesses** **men** **women**

13. *Circle the correct answer.* Iris was the ______________________ of Apollo.

    sister **brother** **son** **daughter**

14. *Read the sentences below. Write 1, 2, 3, 4, or 5 in each blank to show what happened 1st, 2nd, 3rd, 4th, or 5th.*

    ______ Four of the gods had a meeting about Iris.

    ______ The god of the air, the god of the sea, and the god of the rain suggested colors.

    ______ Iris loved the bridge and went to visit the gods and goddesses often.

    ______ The gods wanted to build a bridge for Iris.

    ______ The god of the sun used all the colors to make the bridge.

Read the sentences and questions below. Write the correct sentence in each blank.

She suggested colors for the bridge.
She took messages to other gods and goddesses.
She went to visit her favorite gods and goddesses.
He made a beautiful bridge.
They planned to build a bridge for Iris.

15. What did the god of the sun do? ______________________________

____

____

16. What did Iris do after the bridge was finished? ______________________________

____

____

17. What did Iris do for Apollo? ______________________________

____

____

18. What did the gods do at the meeting? ______________________________

____

____

Read the sentences and phrases below. Check each phrase that correctly completes the sentence.

After Apollo built the bridge, ______________________________.

_____ 19. Iris thought it was beautiful

_____ 20. Iris went to visit her favorite gods and goddesses

_____ 21. the gods had a meeting

_____ 22. Iris was very sad

_____ 23. he gave it to Neptune

_____ 24. the gods suggested colors for it

Read the phrases and sentences below. Fill in each blank with the correct phrase.

because it was beautiful
because that was his favorite color
to talk about Iris
to suggest colors for the bridge
to visit her favorite gods and goddesses
to talk to Neptune

25. The god of the rain suggested indigo ____

____.

26. Iris often went to the sea ____

____.

27. Four of the gods had a meeting ____

____.

28. Iris loved the bridge ____

____.

29. Iris often crossed the bridge ____

____.

Read the sentence and phrases below. Check each phrase that correctly completes the sentence.

The Greek and Roman people believed ____.

______ 30. that the bridge was the first rainbow

______ 31. that this myth was a true story

______ 32. that the gods and goddesses controlled many things on the earth and in the sky

______ 33. that this myth explained something that they did not understand

______ 34. that this myth taught people to build bridges

______ 35. that this myth was not true

AURORA AND TITHONUS

Aurora was the goddess of the dawn. People believed that she controlled the early morning sky. People thought she woke up early to paint the sky with beautiful colors. Some people thought that Aurora came to earth to wake up the flowers and animals.

There once was a boy on earth named Tithonus. He was a very handsome young boy. He loved Aurora dearly. Every night, Tithonus slept in the meadow. He wanted to see Aurora each morning. He waited for her every morning in the green meadow. Aurora loved to see and talk to Tithonus. She thought he was a charming young boy.

One morning Aurora came to work in the meadow. She looked for Tithonus but did not find him. At last, she found him. He was lying on the ground. He was very quiet. He did not move. His eyes were closed and his face was pale.

Aurora was very worried. She walked closer to Tithonus. She picked him up and took him to Mount Olympus. She asked Jupiter for help. Jupiter was the king of the gods and goddesses. He was very strong and very wise. Aurora asked Jupiter to help poor Tithonus. She begged Jupiter to let Tithonus live. She wanted Tithonus to live forever. Jupiter promised Aurora that he would help. He told Aurora that Tithonus would never die.

Aurora took Tithonus back to the meadow. He played and talked again.

Soon something happened. Aurora wanted Tithonus to stay young forever. She forgot to ask Jupiter to let Tithonus stay young. Instead Tithonus began to grow old. After a short time, Tithonus could not walk. His legs began to bend. His knees began to hurt. His face became wrinkled like an old man's face. His skin became dry. His voice changed, too. His voice did not sound like a young boy's voice anymore. His voice sounded like an old man's voice. Tithonus became an old man.

Tithonus was very uncomfortable. He begged for Aurora's help. He told Aurora that he would like to stay in the beautiful green meadow. He told her that he was very happy in the tall, green grass.

So, Aurora changed Tithonus into a grasshopper. She let him go free. She watched him as he jumped away.

The Greek and Roman people believed that Tithonus became the first grasshopper. A grasshopper is a small insect that hops in the tall, green grass in the summer.

AURORA AND TITHONUS
STUDY QUESTIONS

Match the words on the left with the meanings on the right. Write a letter from the right in the correct blank on the left.

______ 1. dawn	a. very kind or very nice
______ 2. charming	b. a noise
______ 3. grasshopper	c. a kind of insect
______ 4. forever	d. parts of the body
______ 5. knees	e. early morning
	f. always

Look at the words below. Then read each sentence. Write the correct word in the blank in each sentence.

bend **pale** **uncomfortable** **wrinkled** **begged** **meadow**

6. Tithonus felt ____________________ when his body changed.

7. Tithonus ________________ Aurora to help him.

8. When Aurora found Tithonus, he had a ____________________ face and his eyes were closed.

9. Tithonus played and talked in the ________________________.

10. When Tithonus began to grow old, his face became ______________________.

11. *Read the words below. Circle the characters from the myth.*

    Apollo **Aurora** **Jupiter** **Tithonus** **Hyacinthus** **Zephyrus**

12. *Circle the correct answer.* Aurora was a ____________________________.

    god **woman** **goddess** **man**

13. *Circle the correct answer.* Tithonus was a ______________________.

    god **girl** **goddess** **boy**

14. *Read the sentences below. Write 1, 2, 3, 4, or 5 in each blank to show what happened 1st, 2nd, 3rd, 4th, or 5th.*

    ______ One day Aurora looked for Tithonus and found him in the meadow.

    ______ Aurora changed Tithonus into a grasshopper.

    ______ Tithonus and Aurora loved each other.

    ______ Tithonus began to grow old and asked Aurora to help him.

    ______ Aurora begged Jupiter to help Tithonus because he did not move.

Read the sentences and questions below. Write the correct sentence in each blank.

She changed him into a grasshopper.
She woke the flowers and animals.
He slept in the meadow.
He changed him into an old man.
He begged Aurora to help him.

15. What did Jupiter do to Tithonus? ______________________________

____

____

16. What did Tithonus do when he became uncomfortable? ______________________________

____

____

17. What did Aurora do to Tithonus? ______________________________

____

____

18. What did Tithonus do every night? ______________________________

____

____

Read the sentence and phrases below. Check each phrase that correctly completes the sentence.

After Tithonus began to grow old, ______________________________.

______ 19. his legs bent and his knees hurt

______ 20. he was very comfortable

______ 21. Aurora went to Mount Olympus

______ 22. his skin was dry and his face became wrinkled

______ 23. his voice sounded like an old man's voice

______ 24. he begged Aurora for help

Read the phrases and sentences below. Fill in each blank with the correct phrase.

because he became an old man
to ask Jupiter for help
because he was uncomfortable
because he wanted to see Aurora each morning
because he was handsome and charming
to wake up the flowers and animals

25. Aurora changed Tithonus into a grasshopper ______________________________

____.

26. Aurora went to Mount Olympus ______________________________

____.

27. Tithonus was uncomfortable ______________________________

____.

28. Aurora came to earth ______________________________

____.

29. Tithonus slept in the meadow ______________________________

____.

Read the sentence and phrases below. Check each phrase that correctly completes the sentence.

The Greek and Roman people believed ______________________________.

______ 30. that this myth was a true story

______ 31. that this myth explained something about nature

______ 32. that Tithonus became the first grasshopper

______ 33. that this myth was not a true story

______ 34. that all old people become grasshoppers

______ 35. that Jupiter made the first grasshopper

EVALUATION
For Section III

PART I - CHARACTERS

Match the names on the left with the phrases on the right. Write the letter of the correct phrase in each blank on the left.

____ 1. Iris
____ 2. Prometheus
____ 3. Neptune
____ 4. Zephyrus
____ 5. Aurora
____ 6. Jupiter
____ 7. Icarus
____ 8. Apollo
____ 9. Hercules
____ 10. Daedalus
____ 11. Tithonus
____ 12. Hyacinthus

a. goddess of the dawn
b. a boy who did not obey
c. god of the sun
d. someone who crossed a rainbow bridge to visit with the gods and goddesses
e. the king of Greece
f. a flower came from this boy's name
g. a famous inventor
h. a Titan who stole fire
i. a young boy who became a grasshopper
j. the name of the wind
k. the king of the gods and goddesses
l. god of the sea
m. a strong man who freed Prometheus

PART II - NOUNS

Write the correct word for each meaning.

island	**rainbow**	**meadow**	**dawn**	**feathers**	**earth**	**flower**	**inventor**
bridge	**fire**	**giants**	**horseshoe**	**torch**	**chains**	**grasshopper**	**voice**

13. ______________: an open field

14. ______________: something that joins two places together

15. ______________: a stick with fire at one end

16. ______________: an insect that can hop

17. ______________: a person who thinks of a new idea

18. ______________: the iron shoe of a horse used to play a game

19. ______________: large, strong humanlike characters

20. ______________: early morning

21. ______________: something that appears in the sky and has seven colors

22. ______________: things that cover a bird's body

23. ______________: a place where people live

24. ______________: an area of land with water around it

25. ______________: something that grows and blooms

26. ______________: heat and light made by something burning

27. ______________: metal circles joined together

PART III - VERBS

Read each sentence. Fill in each blank with the letter of the correct answer.

28. The word *suggested* means________________.

    a. told to do something
    b. told an idea
    c. told someone a joke

29. The word *visit* means________________.

    a. go under the sea
    b. go to see
    c. go to buy

30. The word *chained* means________________.

    a. put into
    b. take apart
    c. held together

31. The word *end* means________________.

    a. went
    b. go
    c. stop

32. The word *crossed* means________________.

    a. went into
    b. went over
    c. went through

33. The word *hop* means________________.

    a. to jump
    b. to run
    c. to walk

34. The word *melt* means________________.

    a. to become strong
    b. to become soft
    c. to become hard

35. The word *protect* means________________.

    a. to ask for danger
    b. to permit danger to come
    c. to keep away from danger

36. The word *suffer* means________________.

    a. to feel pain or sadness
    b. to feel happy
    c. to feel excited

37. The word *drown* means________________.

    a. to die under water
    b. to swim in the water
    c. to sit in the water

38. The word *peck* means________________.

    a. to hit with a large stick
    b. to hit with a bird's beak
    c. to hit with an animal's tail

39. The word *bloom* means________________.

    a. to buy a flower
    b. to plant a flower
    c. to open into a flower

40. The word *escape* means________________.

    a. to ask for permission
    b. to go away without permission
    c. to get something without permission

PART IV - ADJECTIVES

Look at the words below. Then read each sentence. Write the correct word in the blank in each sentence.

strong	**charming**	**large**	**wise**	**dry**	**pale**	**jealous**	**cold**
favorite	**mean**	**good**	**young**	**sharp**	**sad**	**green**	**beautiful**

41. Aurora became worried when she saw Tithonus's ______________________________ face.

42. Zephyrus became ______________________________ of Apollo and Hyacinthus.

43. Grasshoppers hop in tall, ______________________________ grass.

44. Icarus was a ______________________________ man who did not obey his father.

45. Jupiter was a strong and _________________________ god.

46. The Titans were _________________________ giants.

47. Daedalus was ______________________ when his son drowned.

48. The gods made a ____________________________ and beautiful bridge.

49. Some animals have warm fur and _______________________ claws.

50. When Tithonus became old, he had ___________________________ skin.

51. A rainbow has seven ______________________________ colors in it.

52. Aurora thought Tithonus was young and _______________________________.

53. Long ago people had no fire and they were _______________________________.

54. Sometimes Zephyrus was ___________________________________.

55. Iris crossed the bridge to visit her _______________________________ gods and goddesses.

PART V - SEQUENCE

Read the sentences below. Write 1, 2, 3, or 4 in each blank to show what happened 1st, 2nd, 3rd, and 4th.

Daedalus and Icarus

56. ______ Daedalus told Icarus about the sun.
______ Icarus fell into the sea and drowned.
______ Daedalus made some wings.
______ Icarus ignored his father.

Prometheus and the Fire

57. ______ Hercules broke the chains for Prometheus.
______ Prometheus stole fire from the sun.
______ Prometheus wanted to help the people on earth.
______ Jupiter was angry and chained Prometheus to a rock.

Hyacinthus

58. ______ Zephyrus was jealous and hurt Hyacinthus.
______ Some people saw the plant and called it hyacinth.
______ A new plant grew where Hyacinthus died.
______ Hyacinthus and Apollo played horseshoes.

Iris

59. ______ The gods wanted to build a bridge for Iris.
______ Iris crossed the bridge to visit the gods and goddesses.
______ The gods loved Iris so they had a meeting.
______ Apollo made a bridge with seven colors.

Aurora and Tithonus

60. ______ Tithonus began to grow old.
______ Aurora changed Tithonus into a grasshopper.
______ Aurora was worried about Tithonus.
______ Aurora begged Jupiter for help.

PART VI - GREEK AND ROMAN BELIEFS

Read the sentence and phrases below. Check each phrase that correctly completes the sentence.

The Greek and Roman people believed ______________________________________.

______ 61. that myths explained things they did not understand

______ 62. that Iris became a beautiful rainbow

______ 63. that the myth "Daedalus and Icarus" teaches a lesson

______ 64. that sometimes the gods and goddesses helped each other

______ 65. that Hyacinthus became the first flower

______ 66. that some myths teach a lesson

______ 67. that some myths explained about emotions and nature

______ 68. that Tithonus became a grasshopper

______ 69. that myths were not true

______ 70. that Prometheus made the first fire

SECTION IV

MYTHS ❖ GROUP THREE

GLOSSARY

PEGASUS AND BELLEROPHON

1. to agree (agreed)	to decide to do something
2. bolt	a flash of lightning
3. bridle	leather straps put on a horse's head to control the horse
4. to capture	to take by force
5. to conquer	to defeat; to overcome
6. deeds	jobs or acts
7. fangs	long, pointed teeth
8. hero	a special person who does things to help others
9. to roam	to go from place to place
10. temple	a place built to honor a god or goddess
11. thrilled	very happy; excited

MINERVA AND ARACHNE

1. to boast (boasted)	to brag
2. challenge	to ask someone to have a contest
3. contest	a game that has a winner
3. disguise	a costume that makes a person look different
4. to disguise (disguised)	to put on a costume
5. designs	pictures
6. furious	very angry
7. looms	machines used for weaving cloth
8. to mock (mocked)	to make fun of
9. to weave (wove)	to make cloth with many threads or yarn
10. weaver	a person who uses a loom to make cloth from thread or yarn
11. webs	spiders' homes
12. weed	a useless plant

PHAETHON

1. to glare (glared)	to look at someone with anger
2. to greet (greeted)	to welcome; to meet
3. harness	straps used to attach a horse to a cart
4. journey	a long trip
5. nervous	worried
6. palace	a very fine, large house
7. to realize (realized)	to know
8. to rear	to stand on back legs
9. reins	straps joined to a bridle that are held by a driver
10. robes	long, loose pieces of clothing that are often expensive
11. throne	a special chair for a very important person

THE HUNDRED-EYED ARGUS

1. clever	having good ideas; quick to think
2. cloak	a kind of coat
3. to deceive	to trick; to fool
4. depressed	very sad; upset
5. entire	whole; complete
6. to flirt (flirted)	to pay attention to someone so that person will fall in love with you
7. flute	a long, thin musical instrument that makes a sound like a whistle
8. relaxed	comfortable
9. shepherd	a person who takes care of sheep
10. sword	a weapon with a long blade

HOW THE CITY WAS NAMED

1. blooms	flowers
2. buds	flowers that are partly opened
3. capital	a city where the government is located
4. fragrant	smelling sweet
5. fountains	containers that hold water and force it into the air
6. to honor	to show respect for
7. to remain	to stay
8. ripe	ready to pick and eat
9. swift	fast

PEGASUS AND BELLEROPHON

Long ago, a terrible monster lived in the country of Lycia. This monster was called the Chimaera and had the head of a lion, the body of a goat, and the tail of a dragon. It breathed fire and had sharp claws and fangs. The Chimaera caused trouble for everyone, and no one could conquer it.

The king of Lycia asked Bellerophon, a brave young man, to kill the Chimaera. Bellerophon agreed to help the king, but he did not know what to do. He went to the temple of Minerva, the goddess of wisdom, and asked her to help him.

Minerva said to Bellerophon, "I will give you a golden bridle. Go to the meadow and capture Pegasus. Pegasus is the wild white horse with wings that can fly. You must use the magic bridle to ride Pegasus. You and Pegasus can fight the Chimaera together."

Bellerophon was thrilled, for no man had ever ridden Pegasus. He would be the first person to ride the horse.

The next morning, Bellerophon found Pegasus in the meadow. He put the bridle on Pegasus and then jumped onto the horse's back. The horse flew into the air.

Bellerophon and Pegasus flew to the mountain where the Chimaera lived. As Pegasus flew near the monster, Bellerophon shot many arrows into the Chimaera. The monster soon died.

When the people in Lycia heard the news, they were very happy. The king called Bellerophon a hero. Bellerophon and Pegasus did many more brave deeds together, and Bellerophon became famous. He felt very proud and important.

Bellerophon became curious about the gods and goddesses and wanted to see them. One day, he jumped on Pegasus and flew to Mount Olympus, the home of the gods and goddesses. The gods and goddesses were upset because they didn't like people to visit Mount Olympus without permission. Jupiter became angry and caused Pegasus to throw Bellerophon from his back. Bellerophon fell to earth and was hurt badly. He was not able to walk well for the rest of his life. The gods and goddesses forced him to roam the world alone. He never saw Pegasus again. Jupiter kept Pegasus on Mount Olympus to carry his bolts of lightning.

The Greek and Roman people believed that there was a lesson in this myth. They believed that if they acted too proud, they would look foolish or have bad luck.

PEGASUS AND BELLEROPHON
STUDY QUESTIONS

Match the words on the left with the meanings on the right. Write a letter from the right in the correct blank on the left.

____ 1. temple	a. to wander; to go from place to place
____ 2. thrilled	b. acts
____ 3. deeds	c. leather straps put on a horse's head to control the horse
____ 4. roam	d. a place built to honor a god or a goddess
____ 5. bridle	e. wanting to know
	f. very happy

Look at the words below. Then read each sentence. Write the correct word in the blank in each sentence.

fangs **conquer** **fell** **curious** **agreed** **hero**

6. Bellerophon killed the Chimaera and became a ________________________.

7. The king of Lycia wanted Bellerophon to ________________________ the Chimaera.

8. Bellerophon was hurt badly when he ________________________ off of Pegasus.

9. Bellerophon went to Mount Olympus because he was ______________________________.

10. Bellerophon ________________________ to fight the monster.

Read each sentence below. Then circle any words that complete the sentence correctly.

11. The characters in this myth are ________________________.

Minerva **Lycia**

Bellerophon **Olympia**

king **Pegasus**

12. Minerva was a ________________________.

woman **goddess** **man** **god**

13. Bellerophon was a ________________________.

woman **goddess** **man** **god**

Look at the sentences below. Then read the questions. Write the letter of the correct answer to each question in the blank.

a. She gave him a golden bridle.
b. He went to help Jupiter on Mount Olympus.
c. He rode on Pegasus.
d. He shot arrows into it.
e. He caused Pegasus to throw Bellerophon.

14. What did Jupiter do when he became angry? ________

15. What did Minerva do when Bellerophon came to her temple? ________

16. What did Pegasus do after Bellerophon fell? ________

17. What did Bellerophon do to the Chimaera? ________

Read the phrases and sentences below. Fill in each blank with the letter of the correct phrase.

a. because the king of Lycia asked him for help
b. because he went to Mount Olympus
c. to capture Pegasus
d. to ask for help
e. because he killed the Chimaera
f. to carry Jupiter's bolts of lightning

18. Bellerophon became a hero ________.

19. Bellerophon killed the Chimaera ________.

20. Minerva gave Bellerophon the golden bridle ________.

21. Jupiter punished Bellerophon ________.

22. Bellerophon went to the temple ________.

Read the sentences below. Write 1, 2, 3, 4, or 5 in each blank to show what happened 1st, 2nd, 3rd, 4th, and 5th.

23. ______ Bellerophon became proud and thought he was important.

______ The king of Lycia asked Bellerophon to kill a terrible monster.

______ The gods and goddesses punished Bellerophon because he went to Mount Olympus.

______ Minerva gave Bellerophon a bridle to capture Pegasus.

______ Bellerophon and Pegasus went to a mountain to kill the Chimaera.

Read the sentence and phrases below. Check each phrase that correctly completes the sentence.

After Bellerophon fell, he ____.

______ 24. helped Jupiter

______ 25. was not able to walk well

______ 26. went to Mount Olympus

______ 27. had to roam the world alone

______ 28. never saw Pegasus again

______ 29. killed the Chimaera

Read the sentence and phrases below. Check each phrase that correctly completes the sentence.

The Greek and Roman people believed ____________________________________.

______ 30. that this myth explained something they did not understand

______ 31. that this myth was a true story

______ 32. that this myth explained something about nature

______ 33. that this myth taught a lesson

______ 34. that sometimes the gods and goddesses punished people on earth

______ 35. that this myth was not a true story

MINERVA AND ARACHNE

The best weaver in the world was Arachne, a beautiful woman who lived on earth. She worked every day on her weaving and made lovely designs in the things she wove. Some of the designs were of birds, flowers, butterflies, mountains, and trees.

Many forest animals and people on earth came to watch Arachne weave. They thought that Minerva, the goddess of wisdom, had taught Arachne how to weave. When Arachne heard this, she boasted, "Oh, no! Minerva isn't as skillful as I am. Minerva should be asked to prove that she is a good weaver."

When Minerva heard of this, she became angry. She disguised herself as an old woman and went to Arachne's house. She warned Arachne, "Your designs are lovely, but you shouldn't boast so much. You must not try to be better than the goddess Minerva."

Arachne laughed. "I'm not afraid of Minerva," she said. "I will challenge Minerva to a weaving contest. Then all of the people and all of the animals will see who is the more skillful weaver."

The old woman looked surprised and took off her disguise. All of the animals and people bowed because then they knew that the old woman was really Minerva. Arachne also knew that the old woman was Minerva, but she wasn't afraid of her.

Arachne said, "I know that I'm the best weaver in the world. I challenge you to a weaving contest."

Minerva became furious and announced to the people, "Let the contest begin!"

Minerva and Arachne set up their looms and began to weave beautiful things. Minerva wove pictures that told stories about the gods and goddesses. Her pictures showed the gods and goddesses doing brave and wonderful things. Arachne, however, wove pictures that mocked the gods and goddesses. Her pictures told silly stories about the gods and goddesses.

Finally, the two weavers finished their work. The forest animals and the people looked at the pictures the two weavers had woven. They liked the stories.

Minerva carefully studied Arachne's work. She knew that Arachne was a skillful weaver, but she didn't like the stories because they mocked the gods and goddesses. Minerva became angry at Arachne and tore her work into small pieces.

Then Minerva pulled a weed from the ground. She took the juice of the weed and threw it on Arachne. Arachne grew smaller, and her arms and legs became wrinkled. She became a small, ugly gray spider. She was no longer a beautiful woman.

Minerva ordered that Arachne be put into someone's home where she could weave her webs every day. Arachne was an ugly spider for the rest of her life.

The Greeks and the Romans believed that Arachne became the first spider and wove the first webs. Today, the word *arachnid* is used in science to describe small animals with eight legs such as spiders and scorpions. The word *arachnid* comes from the Greek word *arachne*.

MINERVA AND ARACHNE
STUDY QUESTIONS

Match the words on the left with the meanings on the right. Write a letter from the right in the correct blank on the left.

______ 1. weaver	a. to put on a costume
______ 2. disguise	b. spiders' homes
______ 3. webs	c. a machine used for weaving
______ 4. furious	d. a person who makes cloth on a loom
______ 5. challenge	e. very angry
	f. to ask someone to have a contest

Look at the words below. Then read each sentence. Write the correct word in the blank in each sentence.

contest **designs** **mocked** **weed** **wrinkled** **looms**

6. Minerva wove ______________________ of flowers and mountains.

7. Arachne and Minerva wove their designs on ______________________________.

8. Arachne made designs that ___________________________ the gods and goddesses.

9. Minerva and Arachne had a ________________________ to pick the better weaver.

10. When Arachne became small, she had _________________________ arms and legs.

Read each sentence below. Then circle any words that complete the sentence correctly.

11. The characters in this myth are __________________________________.

    Apollo **people**

    Minerva **Mercury**

    Arachne **animals**

12. Arachne was a___________________________.

    god **woman** **goddess** **man**

13. Minerva was a __________________________.

    god **woman** **goddess** **man**

Look at the sentences below. Then read the questions. Write the letter of the correct answer to each question in the blank.

a. She made webs every day.
b. She threw juice from a weed on her.
c. She mocked the gods and goddesses.
d. She tore the work into small pieces.
e. She disguised herself as an old woman.

14. What did Minerva do to Arachne? ________

15. What did Minerva do when she saw Arachne's designs? ________

16. What did Arachne do after she became a spider? ________

17. What did Minerva do before she went to Arachne's house? ________

Read the phrases and sentences below. Fill in each blank with the letter of the correct phrase.

a. because she was not afraid of Minerva
b. to pick the better weaver
c. because she thought that she was a better weaver than Minerva
d. to weave designs
e. because she mocked the gods and goddesses
f. because she was a beautiful woman

18. Minerva and Arachne set up their looms ________.

19. Minerva and Arachne had a contest ________.

20. Minerva changed Arachne into a spider ________.

21. Arachne laughed ________.

22. Arachne boasted ________.

Read the sentences below. Write 1, 2, 3, 4, or 5 in each blank to show what happened 1st, 2nd, 3rd, 4th, and 5th.

23. ______ Minerva wove beautiful pictures of the gods and goddesses.

______ Arachne became a small, ugly spider.

______ Arachne wove pictures that mocked the gods and goddesses.

______ Arachne challenged Minerva to a contest.

______ Minerva did not like Arachne's designs and threw the juice of a weed on her.

Read the sentence and phrases below. Check each phrase that correctly completes the sentence.

After Minerva saw Arachne's designs, she ____.

______ 24. tore the pictures into small pieces

______ 25. became a spider

______ 26. challenged Arachne to a contest

______ 27. threw the juice of a weed on Arachne

______ 28. became angry

______ 29. disguised herself as an old woman

Read the sentence and phrases below. Check each phrase that correctly completes the sentence.

The Greek and Roman people believed ____.

______ 30. that this myth explained emotions

______ 31. that this myth was not a true story

______ 32. that Arachne was the first spider

______ 33. that this myth explained something about nature

______ 34. that all people could weave well

______ 35. that this myth was a true story

PHAETHON

Apollo, the god of the sun, and Clymene, a young woman on earth, had a son named Phaethon. Phaethon lived on earth with his mother while Apollo lived on Mount Olympus with the other gods and goddesses.

Apollo drove a large chariot pulled by wild white horses. Apollo was the only god or goddess strong enough to control the horses. Every day Apollo carried the sun across the sky in his chariot from the east to the west.

Phaethon and his mother often talked about Apollo. Phaethon was very proud of his father and often boasted about him to his friends. Phaethon's friends became tired of his boasting and told Phaethon that they didn't believe Apollo was his father. The boys laughed at Phaethon. Phaethon became angry and shouted, "I can prove that Apollo is my father! I'll go to see him and drive his chariot and horses across the sky for all the world to see."

Phaethon then rushed home to talk to his mother, Clymene. He told her about the boys. He said, "I must prove that Apollo is my father. I want to drive his chariot across the sky so the boys will see me and no longer laugh at me."

Clymene replied, "Travel to the east and meet your father. Be very careful. It is a long journey, and you will be alone."

Phaethon traveled for many days. He walked over mountains and through many forests. Finally, he arrived at his father's palace. When Phaethon went inside, he saw a beautiful, brightly colored room. Apollo was sitting on a huge throne at one end of the room. He was dressed in red and purple robes.

Apollo greeted his son and asked, "Why have you come to my palace?"

Phaethon replied, "My friends laugh at me because they don't believe that you are my father. I must prove that you are my father by doing something important."

Apollo said, "Of course, my son. I will let you do anything."

Phaethon became nervous. He took a deep breath and said, "I want to drive the horses that pull the sun chariot across the sky."

Apollo was shocked when he heard this. He glared at his son and said, "You are my son. I love you very much, but you are a foolish boy. No one else can drive my chariot. No one is strong enough to control the wild white horses. I don't want anyone to mock you, so I will let you try. This will be very dangerous for you."

Phaethon and his father went to get the horses. The horses were bigger than any on earth. They were as white as snow and extremely wild.

As Apollo put a harness on each horse, he warned Phaethon, "Hold the reins tightly. Do not go too high in the sky or you will burn the homes of the gods and goddesses. Do not go too low or you will burn the homes on earth."

Phaethon was very excited and didn't listen carefully to his father. He got into the chariot and started to drive the horses. He saw beautiful colors in the sky and felt the wind on his face. He felt brave and important.

The horses soon realized that Apollo was not their driver. They also knew that Phaethon was weak. They ran faster and faster. Then they began to jump and rear. Phaethon realized that he had lost control of the horses, and he became frightened.

The horses and the chariot with the sun flew low to the earth and touched the people and their homes. The cities and the fields on earth burned. The people on earth called on Jupiter, the king of the gods and goddesses, to help them.

Jupiter was angry with Phaethon and threw a bolt of lightning at him. Phaethon fell from the chariot into the ocean and died. Jupiter saved part of the earth from burning.

The Greek and Roman people believed that this myth explained why there are deserts on earth. Deserts are hot, dry places with few trees and plants. The Greeks and Romans believed that the burned cities and fields on earth became deserts.

PHAETHON
STUDY QUESTIONS

Match the words on the left with the meanings on the right. Write a letter from the right in the correct blank on the left.

______ 1. glared	a. straps used to attach a horse to a cart
______ 2. greeted	b. a long trip
______ 3. harness	c. hurried
______ 4. nervous	d. welcomed
______ 5. journey	e. looked at someone in anger
	f. worried

Look at the words below. Then read each sentence. Write the correct word in the blank in each sentence.

throne **rear** **reins** **robes** **realized** **palace**

6. Phaethon lost control of the horses when they began to jump and ________________ .

7. Phaethon traveled to Apollo's ____________________ .

8. Phaethon pulled the ________________ , but he was not strong enough to control the horses.

9. Apollo wore purple and red ____________________.

10. The horses __________________________ that Phaethon was weak.

Read each sentence below. Then circle any words that complete the sentence correctly.

11. The characters in this myth are ______________________________.

Apollo **Jupiter**

Minerva **Phaethon**

boys **Clymene**

12. Apollo was a _____________________.

woman **goddess** **boy** **god**

13. Phaethon was a _____________________ .

woman **goddess** **boy** **god**

Look at the sentences below. Then read the questions. Write the letter of the correct answer to each question in the blank.

a. They ran faster, and began to jump and rear.
b. They laughed at him.
c. He talked with his wife.
d. He threw a bolt of lightning at Phaethon.
e. He tried to drive the sun chariot across the sky.

14. What did Phaethon do to prove that Apollo was his father? ________

15. What did Jupiter do to help the people on earth? ________

16. What did the boys do when Phaethon boasted about his father? ________

17. What did the horses do when they realized that Phaethon was weak? ________

Read the phrases and sentences below. Fill in each blank with the letter of the correct phrase.

a. to find his mother on earth
b. to prove that Apollo was his father
c. because they laughed at him
d. because he was weak
e. because he was so excited
f. because the cities and fields on earth burned

18. Jupiter was angry at Phaethon ________.

19. Phaethon wanted to drive the sun chariot ________.

20. Phaethon did not listen to his father ________.

21. Phaethon became angry at the boys ________.

22. Phaethon lost control of the horses ________.

Read the sentences below. Write 1, 2, 3, 4, or 5 in each blank to show what happened 1st, 2nd, 3rd, 4th, and 5th.

23. ______ Phaethon wanted to prove that Apollo was his father.

______ Phaethon lost control of the horses and burned the homes and fields on earth.

______ Apollo warned Phaethon about the horses, but Phaethon did not listen.

______ Phaethon boasted to his friends about his father, Apollo.

______ Phaethon told Apollo that he wanted to drive the sun chariot.

Read the sentence and phrases below. Check each phrase that correctly completes the sentence.

After Phaethon lost control of the horses, ____.

______ 24. he fell from the chariot and died

______ 25. the people asked Jupiter for help

______ 26. the cities and fields on earth burned

______ 27. Clymene saved him

______ 28. he felt brave and important

______ 29. Jupiter became angry and threw a bolt of lightning at Phaethon

Read the sentence and phrases below. Check each phrase that correctly completes the sentence.

The Greek and Roman people believed ____.

______ 30. that this myth explained how deserts were formed

______ 31. that this myth was a true story

______ 32. that this myth was not a true story

______ 33. that Apollo controlled the sun

______ 34. that this myth explained something about nature

______ 35. that this myth explained emotions

THE HUNDRED-EYED ARGUS

Jupiter was the king of the gods and goddesses, and Juno was the queen of the gods and goddesses. Sometimes Juno was very jealous because Jupiter thought that other women were beautiful. He liked to flirt with other women. Juno didn't want Jupiter to flirt with other women. She couldn't punish Jupiter because he was king of the gods and goddesses, so she punished the beautiful women instead. She punished them to show Jupiter that he could not deceive her.

Once Jupiter flirted with a beautiful young woman named Io. When Juno learned about Jupiter and Io, she became jealous and angry. She planned to punish Io.

Jupiter liked Io very much and didn't want Juno to punish her. Jupiter wanted to protect Io, so he changed her into a beautiful white cow. Jupiter thought Juno would not find Io and would soon forget her. He planned to change Io into a woman when Juno forgot Io.

Juno, however, was a very wise and clever goddess. She noticed the beautiful white cow near Mount Olympus one day. Juno realized that the cow was really Io. To trick Jupiter, Juno said to him, "Please bring the white cow to me. I want it for a pet."

When Jupiter agreed to give the cow to Juno, she immediately called Argus. Argus was an odd, ugly man who had one hundred eyes. He had eyes on his hands, on his arms, and on his legs and feet. He had eyes on his entire body. The eyes were different colors. Some of them were green, some were blue, and some were brown.

Juno told Argus, "I want you to watch my pet, the white cow. You must always stay with her."

Argus thought he had an easy job. Since he had one hundred eyes, he could watch Io easily.

When Jupiter saw Argus with Io, he became depressed. He felt sorry for Io and wanted to help her. He called Mercury, the messenger of the gods and goddesses, to come to Mount Olympus. Mercury was brave and could run fast. Jupiter told Mercury to kill Argus. Mercury thought that killing Argus would be a very difficult job, but he finally agreed to do the deed.

Mercury disguised himself as a shepherd. He put a sword under his cloak and he carried a flute.

Mercury went to earth to find Argus. He found Argus in a field near the white cow. He began to play sweet music on his flute. Argus listened to the music and did not know the shepherd was Mercury. The music was soft and slow. As Argus became relaxed, his eyes began to close, one by one. Mercury played more music. When he stopped, he looked at Argus. All of Argus's eyes were closed. Argus was asleep!

Mercury quickly jumped up, took his sword, and cut off Argus's head. Argus would not watch Io anymore. Io was now free and happy.

When Juno heard what had happened, she was extremely angry. Juno had liked Argus and was sorry that he was dead. To remember Argus, she collected all of his eyes and took them home. She put one eye on each feather of her peacock's tail. Then she could remember Argus by looking at her peacock.

The Greek and Roman people believed that this myth explained why peacocks have such beautiful tails. A peacock is a large bird that has many large feathers in its long tail. The peacock can spread its tail so that it looks like a fan. The colors of the male peacock's feathers are bright blue, green, and brown. On the end of each feather is a spot that looks like an eye. The peacock's female partner is most often called a peahen. Her colors are not as beautiful or bright as the peacock's colors.

THE HUNDRED-EYED ARGUS
STUDY QUESTIONS

Match the words on the left with the meanings on the right. Write a letter from the right in the correct blank on the left.

______ 1. clever	a. to take care of
______ 2. relaxed	b. comfortable
______ 3. protect	c. very sad
______ 4. deceive	d. a person who takes care of sheep
______ 5. depressed	e. having good ideas
	f. to trick or fool

Look at the words below. Then read each sentence. Write the correct word in the blank in each sentence.

flirted **entire** **cow** **flute** **shepherd** **sword**

6. Mercury disguised himself as a ______________________.

7. Argus had eyes on his ______________________ body.

8. Jupiter ____________________ with many young women.

9. Mercury made Argus sleep by playing a ______________________.

10. Mercury carried a ______________________ and a flute.

Read each sentence below. Then circle any words that complete the sentence correctly.

11. The characters in this myth are ______________________________.

    Mercury **Juno**

    Apollo **Jupiter**

    Argus **Io**

12. Mercury and Jupiter were ___________________________.

    goddesses **gods** **men** **women**

13. Juno was a __________________________.

    goddess **god** **man** **woman**

Look at the sentences below. Then read the questions. Write the letter of the correct answer to each question in the blank.

a. She collected his eyes and put them in her peacock's tail.
b. He changed her into a white cow.
c. He went to earth to catch a cow.
d. He fell asleep.
e. He disguised himself as a shepherd.

14. What did Jupiter do to protect Io? ________

15. What did Argus do when he heard the flute music? ________

16. What did Juno do to remember Argus? ________

17. What did Mercury do to trick Argus? ________

Read the phrases and sentences below. Fill in each blank with the letter of the correct phrase.

a. to protect her
b. to watch Io
c. because Jupiter asked him to do so
d. because the music was sweet
e. because he liked to flirt
f. to trick Argus

18. Jupiter changed Io into a cow ________.

19. Argus fell asleep ________.

20. Mercury disguised himself as a shepherd ________.

21. Juno asked Argus ________.

22. Mercury killed Argus ________.

Read the sentences below. Write 1, 2, 3, 4, or 5 in each blank to show what happened 1st, 2nd, 3rd, 4th, and 5th.

23. ______ Jupiter liked Io and changed her into a cow.

______ Mercury dressed as a shepherd and killed Argus.

______ Juno collected Argus's eyes and put them in her peacock's tail.

______ Jupiter became depressed and asked Mercury to kill Argus.

______ Juno got Io as a pet and asked Argus to watch her.

Read the sentence and phrases below. Check each phrase that correctly completes the sentence.

After Argus died, ____.

______ 24. Io was free

______ 25. Mercury watched Io

______ 26. Juno collected his eyes for the peacock's tail

______ 27. Jupiter married Io

______ 28. he became a cow

______ 29. Juno felt sorry for him

Read the sentence and phrases below. Check each phrase that correctly completes the sentence.

The Greek and Roman people believed ____.

______ 30. that this myth was not a true story

______ 31. that this myth explained the designs on the peacock's tail

______ 32. that this myth explained something about nature

______ 33. that Jupiter controlled peacocks

______ 34. that Juno punished all women

______ 35. that this myth was a true story

HOW THE CITY WAS NAMED

Minerva was the goddess of wisdom. Sometimes people called her by her Greek name, Athena.

Minerva loved one city. Every day she would leave Mount Olympus and visit that city. She thought it was the most beautiful city in the world. There were many water fountains in the center of the city. The gardens in the city had lovely, fragrant flowers and fresh green grass. The trees were tall and the bushes had beautiful blooms. Minerva loved the city dearly.

Neptune, the god of the sea, controlled the rain and the water in the sea. He loved the beautiful city, too. His rain helped the flowers, trees, and bushes to grow. His water also helped the fountains to stay full.

One day Minerva and Neptune went to see Jupiter, the king of the gods and goddesses. Minerva said to Jupiter, "I love that city dearly and want to have it for my own. I will help the people become wise and good. I can teach them to make wonderful things. Please give the city to me."

Neptune, however, became angry. He told Jupiter, "Oh, no! I must have that city for myself. I can help the flowers and trees to grow. I will help the bushes and grass remain green. Then all of the people in the city will be happy. Please give the city to me."

Jupiter replied, "Each of you must choose a wonderful gift for this beautiful city. Bring your gift to me, and I will give the city to the one whose gift is better."

Seven days later, Neptune brought his gift to Jupiter. Neptune brought a beautiful, strong black horse. Neptune told Jupiter, "My gift is the greatest gift. This horse is brave, wise, swift, and strong. Everyone in the city will love this horse, and he will become man's best friend."

On the same day, Minerva took a small tree to the city and planted it. It was an olive tree. She asked Jupiter, "Will you please watch the small tree? It will grow and become the most wonderful gift of all."

Soon the tree began to grow. Buds and blossoms began to appear. Then fruit grew on the tree. When the fruit was ripe, Jupiter called the other gods and goddesses to the city. He wanted them to judge the gifts.

Jupiter showed the gods and goddesses the two gifts. First, he showed them the beautiful black horse. All of the gods and goddesses clapped their hands. They thought that Neptune's gift was wonderful. Then Jupiter showed the gods and goddesses the olive tree that Minerva had planted as her gift. Each god and goddess tasted the fruit. They all clapped their hands again. They thought that Minerva's gift was even more wonderful than Neptune's.

Jupiter agreed. "Yes," he said, "the horse is a fine gift to the people of the city, but the olive tree is much better. This tree can give the people food and make them happy. They will be peaceful because they are satisfied."

So Jupiter gave the city to Minerva. Jupiter said to her, "I would like to call the city Athens to honor your Greek name, Athena."

The Greek and Roman people told this story to explain how the city of Athens got its name. It is the beautiful capital of Greece. Many olive trees still grow there, and the city is known for the wise and intelligent people who have lived there.

The Greeks and Romans also believed that this myth explained the meaning of the olive branch. Many people used olive branches to decorate their homes. They would remember Minerva and feel peaceful. Now, the olive branch means peace.

HOW THE CITY WAS NAMED
STUDY QUESTIONS

Match the words on the left with the meanings on the right. Write a letter from the right in the correct blank on the left.

______ 1. honor	a. smelling sweet
______ 2. fragrant	b. flowers
______ 3. swift	c. a place where people live
______ 4. remain	d. fast
______ 5. blooms	e. to stay
	f. to show respect

Look at the words below. Then read each sentence. Write the correct word in the blank in each sentence.

world **olive** **fountains** **capital** **honor** **buds**

6. Jupiter named the city Athens to ______________________________ Minerva.

7. The olive tree had ______________________________ and then fruit.

8. Neptune helped the ______________________________ to stay full.

9. Athens is the ______________________________ of Greece.

10. The best gift was the ______________________________ tree.

Read each sentence below. Then circle any words that complete the sentence correctly.

11. The characters in this myth are ______________________________.

Jupiter **Olympus**

Minerva **Athens**

Greece **Neptune**

12. Neptune and Jupiter were ____________________________.

gods **goddesses** **men** **women**

13. Minerva was a ______________________________.

god **goddess** **man** **woman**

Look at the sentences below. Then read the questions. Write the letter of the correct answer to each question in the blank.

a. He gave the flowers rain to help them grow.
b. He sent them to another country.
c. She planted it in the city.
d. He asked the other gods and goddesses to help him judge the gifts.
e. He named the city Athens.

14. What did Minerva do with the olive tree? ________

15. What did Neptune do to show he loved the city? ________

16. What did Jupiter do when the olive fruit was ripe? ________

17. What did Jupiter do to honor Minerva? ________

Read the phrases and sentences below. Fill in each blank with the letter of the correct phrase.

a. to win the city
b. because she thought it was beautiful
c. because they liked the gifts
d. because her gift was better than Neptune's
e. to honor Minerva
f. because he was angry

18. Minerva went to visit the city every day ________.

19. Neptune and Minerva brought gifts to Jupiter ________.

20. Jupiter named the city ________.

21. The gods and goddesses clapped their hands ________.

22. Jupiter gave the city to Minerva ________.

Read the sentences below. Write 1, 2, 3, 4, or 5 in each blank to show what happened 1st, 2nd, 3rd, 4th, and 5th.

23. ______ Jupiter said, "I will give the city to the one whose gift is better."

______ Jupiter liked the olive tree better than the horse.

______ Neptune and Minerva loved the same city, and each wanted to have it.

______ Jupiter named the city Athens to honor Minerva.

______ Neptune brought a black horse, and Minerva planted an olive tree.

Read the sentence and phrases below. Check each phrase that correctly completes the sentence.

After Neptune and Minerva showed their gifts to Jupiter, ______________________________.

______ 24. Minerva and Neptune had a fight

______ 25. the other gods and goddesses helped to judge the gifts

______ 26. Jupiter named the city Athens

______ 27. the horse ate all of the olives

______ 28. Minerva became queen of the gods and goddesses

______ 29. Jupiter gave the city to Minerva

Read the sentence and phrases below. Check each phrase that correctly completes the sentence.

The Greek and Roman people believed ______________________________.

______ 30. that this myth explained how Athens got its name

______ 31. that this myth was not a true story

______ 32. that Jupiter controlled all olive trees

______ 33. that each god and goddess had a Greek name and a Roman name

______ 34. that the gods and goddesses controlled many things on earth

______ 35. that this myth was a true story

EVALUATION
For Section IV

PART I - CHARACTERS

Match the names on the left with the phrases on the right. Write the letter of the correct phrase in each blank on the left.

____ 1. Juno
____ 2. Arachne
____ 3. Neptune
____ 4. Clymene
____ 5. Io
____ 6. Minerva
____ 7. Mercury
____ 8. Phaethon
____ 9. Jupiter
____ 10. Bellerophon
____ 11. Argus
____ 12. Apollo

a. the god of the sea
b. a man who had one hundred eyes
c. the god who killed Argus
d. the queen of the gods and goddesses
e. Apollo's son
f. a woman who became a spider
g. the god who flirted with Io
h. a woman who became a cow
i. the man who killed the Chimaera
j. the Roman name for Athena
k. the king of Lycia
l. Phaethon's mother
m. the god of the sun

PART II - NOUNS

Write the correct word for each meaning.

designs	**weaver**	**bridle**	**looms**	**robes**	**journey**	**flute**	**shepherd**
weed	**hero**	**throne**	**temple**	**contest**	**fangs**	**webs**	**capital**

13. ______________: a place built to honor a god or goddess

14. ______________: a place where the government is located

15. ______________: a person who takes care of sheep

16. ______________: a special chair for a very important person

17. ______________: a game that has a winner

18. ______________: pictures

19. ______________: a plant that is useless

20. ______________: a person who makes cloth on a machine

21. ______________: machines used for weaving

22. ______________: a long, thin musical instrument

23. ______________: a special person who does good deeds

24. ______________: spiders' homes

25. ______________: long, pointed teeth

26. ______________: a long trip

27. ______________: leather straps put on a horse's head to control it

PART III - VERBS

Read each sentence. Fill in each blank with the letter of the correct answer.

28. The word *challenge* means________________.

    a. to put on a costume
    b. to trick or fool
    c. to ask someone to have a contest

29. The word *rear* means________________.

    a. fool or trick
    b. stand up on back legs
    c. take care of

30. The word *deceive* means________________.

    a. to trick or fool
    b. to go from place to place
    c. to welcome

31. The word *flirted* means ________________.

    a. looked at someone with anger
    b. asked someone to have a contest
    c. paid attention to someone so that person would fall in love

32. The word *conquer* means________________.

    a. to show respect
    b. to defeat; to overcome
    c. to put on a costume

33. The word *realized* means________________.

    a. knew or understood
    b. looked at someone with anger
    c. hurried

34. The word *remain* means________________.
    a. to show respect
    b. to stay
    c. to make fun of

35. The word *roam* means________________.

    a. to go from place to place
    b. to beat
    c. to take care of

36. The word *agreed* means________________.

    a. wandered
    b. decided to do something
    c. stood on back legs

37. The word *mocked* means________________.

    a. asked someone to have a contest
    b. knew
    c. made fun of

38. The word *capture* means________________.

    a. to take by force
    b. to think the same
    c. to welcome

39. The word *honor* means________________.

    a. to show respect for
    b. to put on a costume
    c. to defeat or overcome

40. The word *disguise* means________________.

    a. to stand on back legs
    b. to put on a costume
    c. to make fun of

PART IV - ADJECTIVES

Look at the words below. Then read each sentence. Write the correct word in the blank in each sentence.

furious swift entire curious fragrant deep clever depressed
jealous nervous wrinkled thrilled relaxed skillful famous weak

41. Bellerophon was ________________________, so he went to Mount Olympus.

42. Arachne became smaller, and her arms and legs became _________________________.

43. Neptune brought a strong, _________________________black horse to Jupiter.

44. Jupiter became _____________________________ because he felt sorry for Io.

45. Bellerophon became ____________________________ because he did brave deeds with Pegasus.

46. Juno knew the cow was Io because Juno was wise and ______________________________.

47. Minerva was _______________ because Arachne boasted that she was the best weaver in the world.

48. When the horses realized that Phaethon was _________________________ , they ran faster.

49. Argus became __________________________ when he heard the flute music.

50. The gardens in Athens had lovely, __________________________ flowers.

51. Phaethon felt _____________________ when he asked to drive the horses that pulled the sun chariot.

52. Juno was angry and ________________________ because Jupiter flirted with Io.

53. Bellerophon was ________________________ because he was the first man to ride Pegasus.

54. Both Arachne and Minerva were ____________________________ weavers.

55. Argus had eyes on his ________________________ body.

PART V - SEQUENCE

Read the sentences below. Write 1, 2, 3, or 4 in each blank to show what happened 1st, 2nd, 3rd, and 4th.

Pegasus and Bellerophon

56. ______ The gods and goddesses punished Bellerophon.
______ Bellerophon and Pegasus killed the Chimaera.
______ Bellerophon thought he was very important.
______ Minerva gave Bellerophon a bridle to capture Pegasus.

Minerva and Arachne

57. ______ Arachne challenged Minerva to a contest.
______ Minerva changed Arachne into an ugly spider.
______ Arachne wove pictures that mocked the gods and goddesses.
______ Arachne wove pictures of flowers, birds, and trees.

Phaethon

58. ______ Phaethon wanted to drive the sun chariot.
______ Phaethon lost control of the horses and burned the earth.
______ Apollo warned Phaethon about the horses, but Phaethon didn't listen.
______ Phaethon wanted to prove that Apollo was his father.

The Hundred-Eyed Argus

59. ______ Io became Juno's pet, and Argus watched her.
______ Juno put Argus's eyes in her peacock's tail.
______ Jupiter changed Io into a cow.
______ Mercury killed Argus for Jupiter.

How the City Was Named

60. ______ Neptune and Minerva showed their gifts to Jupiter.
______ Neptune and Minerva wanted to have the same city.
______ Jupiter liked Minerva's gift better than Neptune's.
______ Jupiter called the city Athens.

PART VI - GREEK AND ROMAN BELIEFS

Read the sentence and phrases below. Check each phrase that correctly completes the sentence.

The Greek and Roman people believed ____.

______ 61. that all cities were named in honor of a god or goddess

______ 62. that myths explained things they did not understand

______ 63. that Arachne became a spider

______ 64. that Argus's eyes became spots on a peacock's tail

______ 65. that Mercury became a peacock

______ 66. that myths were not true

______ 67. that Apollo controlled the sun

______ 68. that Bellerophon was the first flying horse

______ 69. that the myth of Pegasus and Bellerophon teaches a lesson

______ 70. that Athens was named to honor Minerva

SECTION V

MYTHS ❖ GROUP FOUR

GLOSSARY

ECHO AND NARCISSUS

1.	to accept	to believe
2.	cave	a hollow place in a hill or mountain
3.	to disappear (disappeared)	to become invisible; to be out of sight
4.	to refuse (refused)	to say no
5.	to repeat (repeated)	to say again
6.	to respond (responded)	to answer
7.	rushing	moving fast
8.	stream	a small river
9.	to wade (waded)	to walk through water

CLYTIE

1.	beneath	under
2.	coral	pink or red bones of tiny sea animals that are often used for jewelry
3.	dolphins	sea animals that look like small whales
4.	huge	very large
5.	island	a small area of land surrounded by water
6.	nymph	a goddess of nature who lives in seas, rivers, hills, trees, or mountains
7.	pearls	jewels that are found in oysters
8.	roots	parts of a plant that usually grow in the ground
9.	to stare (stared)	to look at for a long time
10.	surface	top

ATLAS

1.	to destroy	to damage; to ruin
2.	difficult	hard
3.	muscles	parts of the body that show strength
4.	pad	a soft pillow used to protect something
5.	to pour (poured)	to flow
6.	to search (searching)	to look for something
7.	shoulders	parts of the body where the arms are attached
8.	sore	hurt
9.	sweat	moisture that comes out of the skin when a person is hot
10.	to tumble	to fall

ORION

1.	aim	ability to hit a target
2.	deep	strong; great
3.	to escape (escaped)	to become free
4.	to miss (missed)	to shoot at something but not hit it
5.	power	a special ability to do something
6.	scorpion	a kind of arachnid having a poisonous sting
7.	skillful	able to do something well
8.	to rise (rose)	to go up
9.	target	something a person shoots at

SATURN

1.	anxious	eager; excited
2.	to banish (banished)	to force someone to leave a place
3.	behavior	the way someone acts
4.	celebration	a big party
5.	exchanging	giving
6.	feasting	eating large amounts of different foods
7.	to harvest (harvested)	to gather crops
8.	to offer (offered)	to present; to give
9.	overjoyed	very happy
10.	vineyards	places where grapes grow

ECHO AND NARCISSUS

Cupid, the young god of love, carried many arrows that he would shoot at people. Some of Cupid's arrows caused people to fall in love. Other arrows caused people to hate each other.

One warm summer day, a young woman named Echo was walking in the forest. Cupid saw Echo and shot her with a love arrow. Echo did not know that she had been shot and did not feel the arrow in her heart.

Soon Echo arrived at a rushing stream. Since she did not see a bridge, she wondered how she could get to the other side of the stream. As Echo thought about her problem, she saw a handsome young man on the other side of the stream. The young man's name was Narcissus.

All of a sudden, Echo was full of love for Narcissus. Cupid's arrow had caused her to fall in love with him. Echo became so excited about meeting Narcissus that she jumped into the rushing water and waded across the stream.

Narcissus, however, had not been hit with one of Cupid's arrows. He did not want to meet her. He yelled at Echo, "Go away! I don't like you! Do not come near me."

"Come near me," repeated Echo.

"Never!" shouted Narcissus. "Stop thinking that I love you!"

"I love you," Echo responded.

Narcissus became more and more angry. He told Echo to go away, but she refused. He told her he did not love her, but she did not accept what he said. Each time Narcissus said something to Echo, she would repeat some of his words. As time passed, she repeated everything he said. She always wanted to be the person who spoke last.

Finally, Narcissus left Echo in the forest by herself. Echo wandered unhappily in the forest until she saw a cave. She decided to go into the cave to be alone with her thoughts. Every day that Echo stayed in the cave, she became more and more depressed about Narcissus. She did not eat or sleep. Soon she became very weak and thin. Echo became so thin and weak that her body disappeared and only her voice was left. People could not see Echo, but they could still hear her voice.

The Greek and Roman people believed that this myth explained the first echo. Echoes can be heard in many places. You can hear an echo if you are in a large and empty room, between many huge buildings, near the mountains, or in a deep valley. If you make a sound in one of those places, you will hear the sound repeated in one or two seconds. You will hear the echo of the sounds you make. For example, you might yell the word "hello" toward the mountains. Soon, you would hear "hello, hello, hello" coming from the mountains. The Greek and Roman people believed that Echo would hide in places and repeat people's words.

ECHO AND NARCISSUS
STUDY QUESTIONS

Match the words on the left with the meanings on the right. Write a letter from the right in the correct blank on the left.

______ 1. voice	a. moving fast
______ 2. rushing	b. to say again
______ 3. refuse	c. sound made through the mouth
______ 4. stream	d. a small river
______ 5. accept	e. to believe
	f. to say no

Look at the words below. Then read each sentence. Write the correct word in the blank in each sentence.

cave **repeated** **disappeared** **weak** **forest** **waded**

6. As time passed Echo ____________________ everything Narcissus said.

7. Echo went to a ____________________ to be alone.

8. Echo ____________________ across a stream to see Narcissus.

9. Echo became thin and ____________________ because she did not eat or sleep.

10. Echo's body ____________________, but people could hear her voice.

Read each sentence below. Then circle any words that complete the sentence correctly.

11. The characters in this myth are ______________________________.

    Cupid **Narcissus**

    Echo **Neptune**

    Io **Apollo**

12. Cupid was a ______________________________.

    goddess **god** **boy** **girl**

13. Echo was a ______________________________.

    goddess **god** **man** **woman**

Look at the sentences below. Then read the questions. Write the letter of the correct answer to each question in the blank.

a. She repeated his words.
b. She became depressed, weak, and thin.
c. He disappeared.
d. He became angry and told her to go away.
e. He shot her with a love arrow.

14. What did Echo do each time Narcissus spoke? ________

15. What did Cupid do to Echo? ________

16. What did Narcissus do when Echo talked about love? ________

17. What did Echo do in the cave? ________

Read the phrases and sentences below. Fill in each blank with the letter of the correct phrase.

a. because she was so weak and thin
b. to have a home in the water
c. because Cupid shot her with a love arrow
d. to be alone
e. because she wanted to be the person who spoke last
f. because Cupid did not hit him with a love arrow

18. Echo went to the cave ____.

19. Echo fell in love with Narcissus ____.

20. Echo disappeared ____.

21. Echo repeated what Narcissus said ____.

22. Narcissus did not love Echo ____.

Read the sentences below. Write 1, 2, 3, 4, or 5 in each blank to show what happened 1st, 2nd, 3rd, 4th, and 5th.

23. ______ Cupid shot a love arrow at Echo.

______ Echo went to a cave to be alone.

______ Echo became weak and her body disappeared, but her voice stayed forever.

______ Narcissus did not love Echo and told her to go away.

______ Echo saw Narcissus and fell in love with him.

Read the sentence and phrases below. Check each phrase that correctly completes the sentence.

After Narcissus left Echo in the forest, she ____.

______ 24. was very happy

______ 25. went to a cave to be alone

______ 26. disappeared and only her voice was left

______ 27. repeated everything he said

______ 28. did not eat or sleep

______ 29. waded in the water

Read the sentence and phrases below. Check each phrase that correctly completes the sentence.

The Greek and Roman people believed ____.

______ 30. that this myth explained something about the first cave

______ 31. that this myth was a true story

______ 32. that Cupid helped all the people on earth

______ 33. that Cupid's arrows were all the same

______ 34. that this myth explained the first echo

______ 35. that this myth was not a true story

CLYTIE

A young sea nymph named Clytie lived in a beautiful palace far beneath the surface of the ocean. There were many lovely sea plants and brightly colored fish around the palace. Clytie wore beautiful jewelry made of coral and pearls. She often rode in a chariot that was made from a huge seashell. There were no horses deep in the ocean so dolphins pulled her chariot. Clytie was very happy in her ocean home.

Early one morning, Clytie decided to visit the earth. She drove her chariot to the surface of the ocean and stopped at an island. As she walked around the island, she noticed the trees and the flowers. She thought that they were beautiful, but she decided that the plants around her palace were even more beautiful. Clytie liked the island, but she decided that her home was even nicer.

The morning sky was a bright red color. Suddenly Clytie saw a huge yellow light in the east. She had never seen anything so bright before. Since she lived in a very dark place far beneath the surface of the sea, she had never seen the sun.

Clytie stared at the light for a long time. Soon, she forgot about her chariot and her wonderful palace in the sea. For nine days, Clytie did not move. She just stood still and watched the sun. She did not eat, and she drank only her tears. She kept her face turned toward the sun.

At last, she could not walk or move because her feet became roots. Her dress changed into green leaves, and her long yellow hair changed into a large yellow flower. Clytie had to remain in the same place forever.

The Greek and Roman people believed that Clytie became the first sunflower, a tall yellow flower that always faces the sun.

CLYTIE
STUDY QUESTIONS

Match the words on the left with the meanings on the right. Write a letter from the right in the correct blank on the left.

______	1. dolphins	a. coral
______	2. huge	b. goddess who lives in seas, rivers, hills, or trees
______	3. nymph	c. sea animals that look like small whales
______	4. beneath	d. very large
______	5. surface	e. top
		f. under

Look at the words below. Then read each sentence. Write the correct word in the blank in each sentence.

palace **coral** **huge** **roots** **gardens** **chariot**

6. When Clytie became a flower, her feet became ______________________________.

7. Clytie lived in a ______________________________ under the sea.

8. Dolphins pulled Clytie's ______________________________ .

9. Clytie's chariot was made of a ______________________________ seashell.

10. Clytie's jewelry was made of ______________________________ and pearls.

Read each sentence below. Then circle any words that complete the sentence correctly.

11. The characters in this myth are ______________________________.

    Apollo **maidens**

    Neptune **chariot**

    Clytie **palace**

12. Clytie was a ______________________________.

    god **man** **nymph** **girl**

13. A sea nymph was a ______________________________.

    goddess **man** **woman** **girl**

Look at the sentences below. Then read the questions. Write the letter of the correct answer to each question in the blank.

a. They pulled her chariot.
b. She stared at the bright light.
c. She made jewelry.
d. She changed into a sunflower.
e. She walked and saw many trees and flowers.

14. What did Clytie do when she saw the sun? ________

15. What did Clytie do when she got to the island? ________

16. What did the dolphins do for Clytie? ________

17. What did Clytie do after staring at the sun for many days? ________

Read the phrases and sentences below. Fill in each blank with the letter of the correct phrase.

a. because she lived far beneath the sea
b. because her feet changed to roots
c. because there were no horses deep in the ocean
d. to make jewelry for the gods and goddesses
e. because she wanted to visit the earth
f. because she had never seen anything that bright before

18. Dolphins pulled the chariot ________.

19. Clytie stared at the sun ________.

20. It was dark near Clytie's palace ________.

21. Clytie rode in her chariot ________.

22. Clytie could not walk ________.

Read the sentences below. Write 1, 2, 3, 4, or 5 in each blank to show what happened 1st, 2nd, 3rd, 4th, and 5th.

23. ______ Clytie stared at the light for nine days and forgot about her home.

______ Clytie fell in love with the sun.

______ Clytie was a nymph who lived in a palace in the ocean.

______ Clytie changed into a sunflower and watched the sun forever.

______ Clytie went to earth to visit.

Read the sentence and phrases below. Check each phrase that correctly completes the sentence.

After Clytie watched the sun for many days, ____.

______ 24. she could not move

______ 25. she forgot about her chariot

______ 26. she rode her chariot back to the palace

______ 27. she went to visit another island

______ 28. she got more beautiful jewelry

______ 29. her feet became roots and her dress became leaves

Read the sentence and phrases below. Check each phrase that correctly completes the sentence.

The Greek and Roman people believed ____.

______ 30. that this myth explained something about emotions

______ 31. that this myth was a true story

______ 32. that this myth was not a true story

______ 33. that this myth explained the first dolphins

______ 34. that this myth explained the first sunflower

______ 35. that this myth taught people to obey their parents

ATLAS

One day, Jupiter asked Hercules, the strong Greek hero, to find some golden apples for him. Although Hercules agreed to do the task, he did not know where to find the golden apples. He asked many gods and goddesses and many people on earth about the golden apples, but no one knew where to find them.

Finally, a very wise man named Prometheus told Hercules to go to the garden of the Hesperides. The Hesperides were young women who lived in a beautiful garden with many fruit trees. Prometheus knew the Hesperides had golden apples in their garden, but he did not know where to find the garden.

Prometheus told Hercules, "You must travel to the end of the world. There you will see a giant named Atlas, who holds the heavens on his shoulders. Atlas is the father of the Hesperides. He will tell you where to find the garden of the golden apples."

Hercules was very excited. He thanked Prometheus and began his journey. After walking for a long time, he arrived at the end of the world. He saw Atlas, the giant, holding the heavens on his shoulders.

Holding the heavens was a difficult job, and Atlas had to do it carefully. If he moved even a little, the stars and the sun might fall onto the earth. If he moved more, the heavens might tumble onto the earth and destroy it. Although Atlas had huge muscles, he was tired from his efforts. Sweat poured from his face. Still, he continued to protect the earth.

Hercules spoke to Atlas. "I am Hercules. Prometheus said that you might help me. I am searching for some golden apples to give to Jupiter, the king of the gods and goddesses. Prometheus said that your daughters have a garden with golden apples. Please tell me where to find their garden."

Atlas responded, "I know where to find their garden, and I will get the apples for you. I'm tired because I have held the heavens for many years. I would like to be free for a short time. If you will hold the heavens for me, I will get the apples for you."

Hercules was pleased with Atlas's idea and agreed to hold the heavens until Atlas returned. Carefully, Atlas gave the heavens to Hercules to hold on his shoulders. Hercules hoped that Atlas would hurry to find the golden apples. The heavens were extremely heavy.

Atlas was gone for a long time. After a while, Hercules became very tired. His shoulders began to hurt, and his back was very sore. He was afraid that he might drop the heavens. He worried that Atlas might never come back and that he would have to hold the heavens forever.

Finally, Atlas came back with the golden apples. Hercules was extremely happy to see Atlas again. He wanted to give the heavens back to Atlas, but Atlas enjoyed being free. Hercules decided to trick Atlas into holding the heavens again.

Hercules said, "I am pleased to hold the heavens for you, but my shoulders are a little sore. I will hold the heavens longer, but first I must make a pad for my shoulders. If you will hold the heavens for a short time, I will make the pad."

Atlas agreed. Then Atlas gave the golden apples to Hercules and Hercules placed the heavens back onto Atlas's shoulders. The trick was successful.

Then Hercules thanked Atlas, said good-bye, and took the golden apples to Jupiter. Atlas had to hold the heavens forever.

The Greek and Roman people believed that a giant named Atlas held the heavens on his shoulders to protect the earth. When people began to make maps of the earth, they wanted to honor Atlas. They used his name on each book of maps. Now the word *atlas* means a book of maps.

ATLAS
STUDY QUESTIONS

Match the words on the left with the meanings on the right. Write a letter from the right in the correct blank on the left.

______ 1. search	a. moisture that comes from the skin when a person is hot
______ 2. sore	b. to damage or ruin
______ 3. destroy	c. to look for something
______ 4. sweat	d. a very large person
______ 5. giant	e. a soft pillow
	f. hurt

Look at the words below. Then read each sentence. Write the correct word in the blank in each sentence.

shoulders **pad** **tumble** **muscles** **pour** **difficult**

6. Hercules wanted to make a ____________________ to protect his shoulders.
7. Atlas was very strong and had huge ____________________ .
8. Atlas moved the heavens onto Hercules's ____________________.
9. It was a ____________________ job to hold the heavens.
10. If Atlas moved, the heavens would ____________________.

Read each sentence below. Then circle any words that complete the sentence correctly.

11. The characters in this myth are____________________.

    Jupiter **Minerva**

    Prometheus **Mercury**

    Atlas **Hercules**

12. Atlas was a ____________________.

    goddess **god** **boy** **giant**

13. The Hesperides were ____________________.

    goddesses **gods** **men** **women**

Look at the sentences below. Then read the questions. Write the letter of the correct answer to each question in the blank.

a. He began his journey to find Atlas.
b. He gave them to Hercules.
c. He went to the garden of the Hesperides.
d. He took the golden apples to Jupiter.
e. He met Prometheus.

14. What did Hercules do after he tricked Atlas? ________

15. What did Atlas do after he gave the heavens to Hercules? ________

16. What did Hercules do after he spoke with Prometheus? ________

17. What did Atlas do with the golden apples? ________

Read the phrases and sentences below. Fill in each blank with the letter of the correct phrase.

a. because he thought Atlas might never come back
b. because he did not want to hold the heavens anymore
c. because they agreed to help each other
d. to find golden apples for Jupiter
e. to protect the earth
f. to make a pad for his shoulders

18. Hercules tricked Atlas ________.

19. Hercules was searching ________.

20. Hercules held the heavens for Atlas ________.

21. Hercules became worried ________.

22. Atlas held the heavens ________.

Read the sentences below. Write 1, 2, 3, 4, or 5 in each blank to show what happened 1st, 2nd, 3rd, 4th, and 5th.

23. ______ Atlas held the heavens forever, and Hercules took the apples to Jupiter.

______ Hercules became tired and worried that Atlas would not return.

______ Hercules asked Atlas to help him find the golden apples.

______ Atlas moved the heavens onto Hercules's shoulders.

______ Hercules tricked Atlas into holding the heavens.

Read the sentence and phrases below. Check each phrase that correctly completes the sentence.

After Hercules tricked Atlas, he ____.

______ 24. thanked Prometheus

______ 25. went to visit the Hesperides

______ 26. went to find the garden

______ 27. took the apples to Jupiter

______ 28. went to see Prometheus

______ 29. thanked Atlas and said good-bye

Read the sentence and phrases below. Check each phrase that correctly completes the sentence.

The Greek and Roman people believed ______________________________________.

______ 30. that Atlas held the heavens to protect the earth

______ 31. that this myth was not a true story

______ 32. that this myth was a true story

______ 33. that this myth explained something about nature

______ 34. that all gods and giants are the same

______ 35. that Hercules married the Hesperides

ORION

One of Neptune's children was a giant named Orion. Orion had two great gifts. He was a skillful hunter, and he had the power to walk on water.

One day, Orion met Diana, the goddess of hunting. They became friends and spent many days hunting together. Both Diana and Orion were very skillful with a bow and arrows.

After a while, Apollo, Diana's brother, became jealous of Diana's deep friendship with Orion. Apollo disliked Orion and worried that Diana might fall in love with him. To make Orion go away, Apollo sent a giant scorpion to fight him. Orion could not kill the strong scorpion with his arrows, his sword, or his club. Finally he escaped the scorpion by walking out onto the sea.

When Apollo learned that the scorpion had not destroyed Orion, he was angry. He decided to trick Diana into killing Orion.

Apollo knew that Diana loved to show her skill with her bow. He asked her to shoot arrows at some rocks in the sea. Each time Diana shot an arrow, it hit a rock. She never missed her target. Then Apollo asked Diana to shoot at a large rock that rose out of the sea far from shore. Her aim was perfect, and Apollo praised her skill.

Soon the waves carried Orion's dead body to the shore where Diana stood. When Diana realized that it was Orion she had shot and not a large rock, she became terribly upset.

She said, "I will never forget my dear friend Orion, and I want the people in the world to remember him, too."

To honor Orion, Diana sent his body up to the heavens. There it changed into a group of bright stars and stayed in the heavens forever.

The Greek and Roman people believed that Orion became an important constellation. A constellation is a group of bright stars that make a picture in the sky at night. The constellation Orion shows the outline of a great hunter with his sword and club. The three brightest stars in the constellation show his belt.

ORION
STUDY QUESTIONS

Match the words on the left with the meanings on the right. Write a letter from the right in the correct blank on the left.

______ 1. power	a. ability to hit a target
______ 2. target	b. special ability to do something
______ 3. skillful	c. strong or great
______ 4. aim	d. to go up
______ 5. rise	e. something a person shoots at
	f. able to do something well

Look at the words below. Then read each sentence. Write the correct word in the blank in each sentence.

aim **power** **target** **scorpion** **deep** **missed**

6. Orion had the ______________________ to walk on water.

7. Apollo was jealous of Diana's ______________________ friendship with Orion.

8. Diana's ______________________ was perfect, and she killed Orion.

9. Diana never missed her ______________________.

10. Orion fought a giant ______________________.

Read each sentence below. Then circle any words that complete the sentence correctly.

11. The characters in this myth are ______________________.

Orion **Diana**

Bacchus **king**

Apollo **Jupiter**

12. Diana was a ______________________.

goddess **god** **man** **woman**

13. Orion was a ______________________.

goddess **god** **man** **giant**

Look at the sentences below. Then read the questions. Write the letter of the correct answer to each question in the blank.

a. He tricked Diana.
b. He became jealous.
c. She changed him into a constellation.
d. She spent many days hunting with him.
e. He walked out onto the sea.

14. What did Diana do to Orion after he died? ________

15. What did Orion do to escape the scorpion? ________

16. What did Apollo do to kill Orion? ________

17. What did Apollo do when he learned of Diana's new friendship? ________

Read the phrases and sentences below. Fill in each blank with the letter of the correct phrase.

a. because he disliked him
b. because she thought he was a rock
c. because he could walk on water
d. to become jealous
e. to remember him
f. because he liked hunting

18. Apollo sent a giant scorpion to fight Orion ________.

19. Orion became a friend of Diana ________.

20. Orion escaped the scorpion ________.

21. Diana shot Orion ________.

22. Diana sent Orion to the heavens ________.

Read the sentences below. Write 1, 2, 3, 4, or 5 in each blank to show what happened 1st, 2nd, 3rd, 4th, and 5th.

23. ______ Orion went hunting with Diana.

______ Orion walked out onto the sea.

______ Orion changed into a constellation, and people could remember him forever.

______ Apollo, Diana's jealous brother, tricked her into killing Orion.

______ Apollo sent a scorpion to kill Orion.

Read the sentence and phrases below. Check each phrase that correctly completes the sentence.

After Orion died, ____.

______ 24. people saw his constellation and would remember him

______ 25. the waves brought his body to shore

______ 26. Apollo tricked Diana

______ 27. he changed into a constellation

______ 28. Diana became upset

______ 29. Diana sent his body to the heavens

Read the sentence and phrases below. Check each phrase that correctly completes the sentence.

The Greek and Roman people believed ____________________________________.

______ 30. that this myth was a true story

______ 31. that Apollo became a constellation

______ 32. that this myth explained something about nature

______ 33. that Orion became a constellation

______ 34. that this myth was not a true story

______ 35. that Orion and Diana were married

SATURN

Saturn, the god of time, lived in the skies. He had many sons and daughters, but he was very mean to them. He thought that his children might grow up to be more powerful than he, so he did terrible things to them.

Jupiter was the only one of Saturn's sons who escaped his father's unkind behavior. When Jupiter grew up to become the king of the gods and goddesses, he decided to punish Saturn for the terrible things he had done. Jupiter banished Saturn to the countryside outside of Rome. Saturn was not permitted to go to Mount Olympus where other gods and goddesses lived. He had to remain on earth.

Saturn was sent to a pleasant land with high mountains and green valleys. The land was rich, and the people of the land were kind to each other.

After he had lived in the countryside for a while, Saturn felt bad about what he had done to his children. He wanted to change his mean behavior, so he decided to help the people of the countryside. Saturn taught the people how to plant crops and to care for their fields and vineyards. Then he showed them how to harvest crops from their fields and vineyards when the crops were ripe. The people were overjoyed at Saturn's helpfulness and kindness.

After they had harvested their crops, the people wanted to honor Saturn for all of his help. They had a celebration that lasted seven days, which they called the Saturnalia. It was a time of great feasting and a time of exchanging gifts. Many people made dolls that looked like Saturn. The people prayed to the gods and goddesses so that Saturn would never leave them. They offered gifts to the gods and goddesses so that Saturn would stay on earth forever.

When the Saturnalia ended, it was time for winter. Then the people would rest and eat the foods that Saturn had taught them to grow. Through the winter months, they were anxious for spring when they would work in the fields and vineyards with Saturn again.

The Greek and Roman people believed that this myth explained why the Saturnalia was named for Saturn. Saturday, the last day in the week, is also named after Saturn. The Saturnalia lasted seven days, so the seventh day of the week is called Saturday. Also, since Saturn once lived in the sky, we now use his name for one of the planets in our solar system.

SATURN
STUDY QUESTIONS

Match the words on the left with the meanings on the right. Write a letter from the right in the correct blank on the left.

______	1. crops	a. extremely mean
______	2. overjoyed	b. eager or excited
______	3. celebration	c. plants grown especially for food
______	4. anxious	d. very happy
______	5. vineyards	e. a big party
		f. places where grapes grow

Look at the words below. Then read each sentence. Write the correct word in the blank in each sentence.

exchanged **offered** **banished** **escaped** **harvested** **honor**

6. The people wanted to ______________________ Saturn during the Saturnalia.

7. Jupiter ______________________ Saturn to the countryside near Rome.

8. The people ______________________ gifts to the gods and goddesses so Saturn could stay.

9. The people ______________________ crops from their fields.

10. Jupiter ______________________ from his father's unkind behavior.

Read each sentence below. Then circle any words that complete the sentence correctly.

11. The characters in this myth are ______________________.

Pluto **people**

Juno **Neptune**

Jupiter **Saturn**

12. Jupiter was a ______________________.

goddess **god** **woman** **man**

13. Saturn was a ______________________.

goddess **god** **woman** **man**

Look at the sentences below. Then read the questions. Write the letter of the correct answer to each question in the blank.

a. They went to visit the gods and goddesses with plates of food.
b. They had a celebration for seven days.
c. He banished him to the countryside.
d. He taught the people about crops and harvesting.
e. They would rest and eat the foods Saturn had taught them to grow.

14. What did Saturn do when he was banished to the countryside? ________

15. What did Jupiter do to punish Saturn? ________

16. What did the people do to honor Saturn? ________

17. What did the people do when the Saturnalia ended? ________

Read the phrases and sentences below. Fill in each blank with the letter of the correct phrase.

a. because they did not want Saturn to leave
b. to change his bad behavior
c. to become the god of time
d. to honor Saturn
e. because of the terrible things he had done
f. because Saturn was kind and helpful

18. The people were overjoyed ________.

19. The people had a celebration for seven days ________.

20. Jupiter banished Saturn to the countryside ________.

21. The people prayed to the gods and goddesses ________.

22. Saturn wanted to help people ________.

Read the sentences below. Write 1, 2, 3, 4, or 5 in each blank to show what happened 1st, 2nd, 3rd, 4th, and 5th.

23. ______ The people wanted to honor Saturn with the celebration called Saturnalia.

______ Saturn was terrible to his children.

______ Saturn taught the people about planting and harvesting crops.

______ Jupiter banished Saturn to the countryside, where Saturn changed his behavior.

______ Jupiter escaped from his father and became the king of the gods and goddesses.

Read the sentence and phrases below. Check each phrase that correctly completes the sentence.

After Saturn taught the people to harvest crops, they ____.

______ 24. offered gifts to the gods and goddesses

______ 25. called Jupiter to help

______ 26. wanted to honor him

______ 27. behaved badly

______ 28. became anxious for spring

______ 29. had a celebration

Read the sentence and phrases below. Check each phrase that correctly completes the sentence.

The Greek and Roman people believed ____.

______ 30. that this myth was a true story

______ 31. that this myth explained the Saturnalia celebration

______ 32. that Jupiter was a terrible god

______ 33. that this myth was not a true story

______ 34. that the gods and goddesses disliked crops

______ 35. that Saturn became the first vineyard

EVALUATION
For Section V

PART I - CHARACTERS

Match the names on the left with the phrases on the right. Write the letter of the correct phrase in each blank on the left.

______ 1. Diana
______ 2. Clytie
______ 3. Jupiter
______ 4. Atlas
______ 5. Apollo
______ 6. Orion
______ 7. Echo
______ 8. Saturn
______ 9. Prometheus
______ 10. Hercules
______ 11. Narcissus
______ 12. Cupid

a. a nymph who became a sunflower
b. a giant who became a constellation
c. a god who tricked Diana
d. a wise man who knew about the Hesperides
e. a young man who did not love Echo
f. a god who asked Hercules to find golden apples
g. a young woman who became weak and disappeared
h. a god who shot Echo with a love arrow
i. a king of an island
j. a god who taught people about crops
k. a goddess who shot Orion
l. a Greek hero who brought golden apples to Jupiter
m. a giant who held the heavens

PART II - NOUNS

Write the correct word for each meaning.

cave	**power**	**giant**	**stream**	**nymph**	**surface**	**dolphins**	**scorpion**
pad	**roots**	**celebration**	**muscles**	**pearls**	**behavior**	**sweat**	**target**

13. _____________: jewels that are found in oysters
14. _____________: a very large person
15. _____________: a kind of arachnid having a poisonous sting
16. _____________: special ability to do something
17. _____________: a soft pillow used to protect something
18. _____________: a hollow place in a hill or mountain
19. _____________: a big party
20. _____________: the way someone acts
21. _____________: sea animals that look like small whales
22. _____________: parts of a plant that usually grow in the ground
23. _____________: parts of the body that show strength
24. _____________: top
25. _____________: moisture that comes out of the skin when a person is hot
26. _____________: a goddess who lives in seas, rivers, hills, or trees
27. _____________: something a person shoots at

PART III - VERBS

Read each sentence. Fill in each blank with the letter of the correct answer.

28. The word *destroy* means__________________.

    a. to damage; to ruin
    b. to say again
    c. to answer

29. The word *refuse* means__________________.

    a. to fall
    b. to say again
    c. to say no

30. The word *stared* means__________________.

    a. looked at for a long time
    b. answered
    c. forced someone to leave a place

31. The word *offered* means__________________.

    a. believed
    b. presented; gave
    c. became invisible; was out of sight

32. The word *waded* means__________________.

    a. walked through water
    b. shot at something but didn't hit it
    c. went up

33. The word *repeat* means__________________.

    a. say no
    b. say again
    c. force someone to leave a place

34. The word *disappeared* means_______________.

    a. shot at something but didn't hit it
    b. answered
    c. became invisible; was out of sight

35. The word *escaped* means__________________.

    a. presented; gave
    b. became free
    c. looked at for a long time

36. The word *missed* means__________________.

    a. looked for something
    b. shot at something but didn't hit it
    c. damaged; ruined

37. The word *banished* means__________________.

    a. forced someone to leave a place
    b. believed
    c. walked through water

38. The word *respond* means__________________.

    a. to go up
    b. to say again
    c. to answer

39. The word *search* means__________________.

    a. to look for something
    b. to become free
    c. to say no

40. The word *accept* means__________________.

    a. to present or give
    b. to believe
    c. to become invisible

PART IV - ADJECTIVES

Look at the words below. Then read each sentence. Write the correct word in each blank.

rushing	**young**	**overjoyed**	**skillful**	**sore**	**jealous**	**difficult**	**weak**
handsome	**terrible**	**deep**	**anxious**	**upset**	**huge**	**depressed**	**ripe**

41. Diana and Orion had a ______________________________ friendship.

42. Diana's brother, Apollo, was ______________________________ of Orion.

43. Saturn was so helpful and kind that the people were ______________________________.

44. Echo stopped beside a ______________________________ stream to think.

45. Diana was very ______________________________ when she learned that she had killed Orion.

46. Hercules wanted a pad because his shoulders were ______________________________.

47. Echo disappeared because she became thin and ______________________________.

48. Atlas was strong, but he had a ______________________________ job.

49. Narcissus was a ______________________________ young man.

50. Echo became so ______________________________ that she did not eat or sleep.

51. The Hesperides were ______________________________ women who had golden apples in their garden.

52. Saturn did ______________________________ things to his children.

53. Diana was very ______________________________ with a bow and arrow.

54. The people wanted to work with Saturn, so they were ________________________ for spring to come.

55. Clytie watched a __________________________ yellow light until she became a flower.

PART V - SEQUENCE

Read the sentences below. Write 1, 2, 3, or 4 in each blank to show what happened 1st, 2nd, 3rd, and 4th.

Echo and Narcissus

56. ______ Echo disappeared, but her voice stayed forever.
______ Narcissus told Echo to go away.
______ Echo went to a cave.
______ Echo fell in love with Narcissus.

Clytie

57. ______ Clytie lived in the ocean.
______ Clytie went to earth to visit.
______ Clytie changed into a sunflower.
______ Clytie stared at the sun and forgot her home.

Atlas

58. ______ Hercules worried because Atlas was gone a long time.
______ When Atlas returned, Hercules tricked him.
______ Hercules took the golden apples to Jupiter.
______ Atlas gave the heavens to Hercules to hold.

Orion

59. ______ Diana sent Orion to the heavens to become a constellation.
______ Apollo sent a scorpion to kill Orion.
______ Orion and Diana went hunting.
______ Diana killed Orion because Apollo tricked her.

Saturn

60. ______ Jupiter became king of the gods and goddesses after he escaped from his mean father.
______ Saturn taught the people to plant crops and harvest them.
______ Jupiter banished Saturn, and Saturn changed his behavior.
______ The people wanted to honor Saturn with the celebration called the Saturnalia.

PART VI - GREEK AND ROMAN BELIEFS

Read the sentence and phrases below. Check each phrase that correctly completes the sentence.

The Greek and Roman people believed ______________________________________.

______ 61. that Clytie became the first sunflower

______ 62. that the gods and goddesses were kind to everyone on earth

______ 63. that Narcissus became the first echo

______ 64. that myths were true stories

______ 65. that all constellations are named Orion

______ 66. that Cupid had love arrows and hate arrows

______ 67. that all myths explained something about nature

______ 68. that Atlas held the earth to protect the heavens

______ 69. that myths are not true

______ 70. that the myth about Saturn explained a celebration

SECTION VI

MYTHOLOGY IN MODERN TIMES

USING MYTHOLOGY TODAY

GLOSSARY

1.	influence (influenced)	to use power or control
2.	society	a group of people who have similar beliefs
3.	symbols	something that reminds us of an object or idea
4.	ancient	very, very old; a long time ago
5.	calendar	a list of days, weeks, and months of the year

MYTHOLOGY IN OUR DAILY LIVES

Greek and Roman mythology has influenced our society for many years. If we look around in our daily lives, we can see many ways that people have copied ideas and words from Greek and Roman mythology. We see these ideas and words used on buildings, in books, and at businesses.

It is important to study Greek and Roman mythology so we are familiar with the many ways we now use what we have learned from mythology. There are symbols that we use that come from mythology. There are names that we use that are copied from Greek and Roman names and places.

This section of this book will help you to understand some of the ways that people now use the information from mythology of ancient times. You may find other ways, too. You should share what you find with your teacher, your class, or someone who enjoys learning about new things.

THE MONTHS

Naming the months of the year is one of the ways we have copied ideas and names from Greek and Roman mythology. The names of some months have been copied from the names of gods and goddesses. Others have been copied from names of famous Roman emperors and from Latin words. Latin was the language of the Roman people.

There are twelve months in a year. Most months have 30 or 31 days and one month has only 28 days. We count 365 days each year. Counting the days in a month and the months in each year helps us to keep track of time. Most people use a calendar to count the days in a week and months in a year.

The Roman calendar only had ten months. Our calendar has twelve months. The months are listed below in the order of our calendar. The word from ancient Greek or Roman times that was used to name each month is also listed.

MONTHS	**ORIGINS**
January	Janus, god of doors, beginnings, sunset, sunrise
February	*februare*: Latin for "to purify"
March	Mars, god of war
April	Aphrodite (Venus), goddess of love and beauty
May	Maia, goddess, mother of Mercury
June	Juno, queen of the gods and goddesses
July	Julius Caesar, Roman emperor
August	Caesar Augustus, Roman emperor
September	*septem*: Latin for "seven"
October	*octo*: Latin for "eight"
November	*novem*: Latin for "nine"
December	*decem*: Latin for "ten"

THE MONTHS
STUDY QUESTIONS

Read each sentence below. Fill in the blank with the correct word.

1. There are ____________________ months in a year.
2. ____________________ was the language of the Roman people.
3. The month of ____________________ is named for Juno, queen of the gods and goddesses.
4. The month of ____________________ is named for Maia, mother of Mercury.
5. A ____________________ is used by some people to count the days and months in a year.
6. ____________________ was the god of doors and beginnings.
7. The month of ____________________ is named for Augustus Caesar.
8. The month of ____________________ is just before the month of March.
9. The month of ____________________ is named for Julius Caesar.
10. The month of ____________________ is just after the month of September.
11. The Latin word *novem* means ____________________.
12. April is named for the Greek goddess of beauty, ____________________.
13. The month of December is named for the Latin word ____________________.
14. There are ____________________ days in a year.
15. The month of ____________________ is named for the Latin word meaning "seven."

SYMBOL STORIES

GLOSSARY

MYTHOLOGICAL SYMBOLS

1. clover	a short plant that grows in fields and lawns
2. gesture	a movement of the body that communicates an idea
3. lyre	a musical instrument that looks like a small harp
4. organization	a group of people who work together for a reason
5. profession	a job; an occupation
6. to represent (represents)	to stand for
7. track and field	a group of sports that includes running and jumping

PHYSICIAN

1. abbreviation	the short form of a word
2. to conduct (conducts)	to direct; to manage
3. conventions	large meetings
4. diseases	illnesses
5. herbs	plants that are used for medicine
6. hospital	a place where sick people get help
7. pharmacies	places where people can buy medicine and medical supplies
8. physician	doctor
9. private practice	a doctor's own business
10. seminars	small meetings
11. staff	a long wooden stick

CUPID

1. appearance	the way a person looks
2. greeting card	a card with a message sent to a person at a special time
3. mention (mentioned)	to talk about
4. mischievous	liking to play tricks
5. quiver	a container that holds arrows

FLORISTS' TRANSWORLD DELIVERY

1. customer	a person who buys something
2. to deliver (delivered)	to bring to a person
3. florists	businesses that sell flowers and plants
4. messenger	a person who delivers something
5. occasions	special times

MUSICIAN

1. argument	a fight; a disagreement
2. harp	a large musical instrument with many strings
3. hobby	something a person does for fun, without getting paid
4. musical instrument	something that makes music
5. to settle	to stop
6. tortoise	a large turtle

THE UNITED NATIONS

1. continents	large areas of land on the earth
2. headquarters	the main office of a business, a club, or an organization
3. nations	areas of land that have governments; countries
4. peace	freedom from war
5. united	joined together

MYTHOLOGICAL SYMBOLS

We remember Greek and Roman mythology in many ways. One way is through the use of mythological symbols.

A symbol is something that reminds us of an object or an idea. A symbol can be a picture, a letter, a sound, a gesture, a word, or an object. We see and use symbols every day. A symbol can represent a sport, a country, an organization, a religion, a profession, or a company. A few common symbols are the eagle for the United States, a heart for love, and a four-leaf clover for good luck.

Symbols that are copied from mythology are called mythological symbols. Some common mythological symbols are a foot with wings for track and field activities, a lyre for music, and an olive branch for peace.

The next five stories tell about some symbols that come from Greek and Roman mythology. The symbols are ones that we see often. They show us that Greek and Roman mythology is still important in our lives.

PHYSICIAN

staff of Aesculapius

In ancient Greece and Rome, over three hundred temples were built to honor Aesculapius, the god of medicine. Aesculapius learned the art of healing the sick from his father, Apollo, and was skillful in using herbs to cure the sick. Many people thought that Aesculapius was the founder of medicine.

The snake was the symbol for Aesculapius and his healing powers. Sick people would bring gifts to the temples of the snake, hoping to become well.

Today, the symbol for physicians is called the staff of Aesculapius. It looks like a staff with a snake around it. The staff of Aesculapius can be seen in hospitals, physicians' offices, pharmacies, and many other places.

caduceus

Physicians can work in a hospital or have a private practice. Physicians can be members of the A.M.A., which is the abbreviation for the American Medical Association. The A.M.A. gives physicians new information about medicine, laws, and diseases. It also conducts seminars and holds conventions. The A.M.A. uses the staff of Aesculapius as part of its symbol.

Another symbol that was used to represent different medical professions is called the caduceus. The caduceus is a staff with wings at the top and two snakes around it. The staff represents good health and quick healing and was copied from the staff of Mercury, the god of speed. The caduceus is no longer used for the A.M.A., but it is still seen today.

CUPID

Cupid was the son of Venus, the goddess of love and beauty. He was very young and handsome and had wings so that he could fly. He carried a small bow and a quiver full of arrows. Cupid often shot people and gods and goddesses with his arrows. Some of his arrows caused people to love, and other arrows caused people to hate. The mischievous Cupid liked to play tricks on people and other gods and goddesses.

Cupid is remembered for his boyish appearance and the way he helped people to fall in love with each other. He is mentioned in many Greek and Roman stories. For example, he shot Echo with a love arrow and caused her to fall in love with Narcissus.

Today, Cupid is a symbol for love. In some countries, people celebrate Valentine's Day every February 14th. It is a special day to remember someone you love by sending a greeting card, buying flowers, or giving candy to that person. We often see pictures of Cupid or hear people speak about him on that day.

FLORISTS' TRANSWORLD DELIVERY

Florists' Transworld Delivery is an organization of florists around the world. F.T.D. is the abbreviation for this organization. Florists who are members of F.T.D. can deliver flowers and plants to people all over the world.

Florists sell plants and flowers for many occasions, such as weddings, funerals, anniversaries, and holidays. Sometimes people go to a florist to buy their flowers or plants. Sometimes people telephone to ask a florist to deliver flowers to homes, churches, or hospitals.

Florists all over the world who belong to F.T.D. cooperate so their customers will be happy. Sometimes a person wants to send flowers to a friend who lives far away. The person can go to a florist that has the F.T.D. symbol in the window of the store. After the person chooses the flowers to send to the friend, the florist calls another florist in the friend's city and orders the flowers. The other florist delivers the flowers to the friend in that city.

The symbol for F.T.D. is a picture of a god who is holding flowers in one hand. The name of the god is Mercury, the messenger of the gods and goddesses. He has wings on his hat and wings on his feet. The Greek and Roman people believed that the wings helped Mercury to travel fast and deliver his messages very quickly. F.T.D. uses this symbol because they deliver flowers quickly to any place in the world.

MUSICIAN

A musician is a person who plays a musical instrument. There are many different kinds of musical instruments. Some musical instruments are the drum, the trumpet, the piano, the flute, the violin, and the guitar.

Musicians play their instruments for many different reasons. Some people enjoy music as a profession and others as a hobby. Some musicians play their instruments in a group called a band. Some people enjoy dancing to band music, and other people like to listen to the music.

The symbol for a musician is the lyre. A lyre is a musical instrument that looks like a small harp. People believed that Mercury found a tortoise shell one day and made a lyre from it. Then Mercury and Apollo, the god of music, had an argument about the instrument. Mercury gave the lyre to Apollo to settle the argument. From then on, Apollo played the lyre for the Greek gods and goddesses. The gods and goddesses enjoyed the music, and the lyre became an important musical instrument for them.

THE UNITED NATIONS

The United Nations is an organization of many different nations. All of the nations in the organization work together for peace. The abbreviation used for the United Nations is U.N. The U.N. has meetings at its headquarters in New York City. Each nation chooses men and women to go to the meetings. Those men and women are called delegates, and the most important delegate from each nation is called an ambassador.

The symbol for the United Nations is a map of the world with an olive branch along each side of the map. The map shows the continents of the world. The delegates to the United Nations come from many of the continents.

The branches of the olive tree are a symbol for peace. Minerva, the goddess of wisdom, gave the olive tree to the city of Athens. The olive tree made the people of Athens happy and gave them food. They did not fight anymore and lived in peace.

The United Nations uses the olive branches in its symbol because it wants everyone in the world to stop fighting. The U.N. wants people to live in peace.

SYMBOL STORIES
STUDY QUESTIONS

Match the words on the left with the meanings on the right. Write the letter of the correct meaning in each blank on the left.

______ 1. florists	a. the main office of a business, club, or organization
______ 2. headquarters	b. a person who plays a musical instrument
______ 3. pharmacies	c. people who buy something
______ 4. customers	d. businesses that sell flowers and plants
______ 5. musician	e. large meetings
	f. places where people can buy medicine and supplies

Look at the words below. Then read each sentence. Write the correct word in the blank in each sentence.

conducts **settle** **deliver** **symbol** **represent**

6. Florists ____________________ flowers to customers.

7. Cupid is a ____________________ for love.

8. A symbol can ____________________ an object or an idea.

9. Mercury tried to ____________________ an argument.

10. The American Medical Association ________________________ seminars for physicians.

Read the words below. Write the correct answer in each blank.

United Nations **F.T.D.** **physician** **musician** **love**

11. The staff of Aesculapius is the symbol for a ________________________.

12. The map of the world with an olive branch is the symbol for the ________________________________.

13. A lyre is the symbol for a ___________________________.

14. Cupid is the symbol for ____________________________.

15. Mercury holding some flowers is the symbol for ____________________________.

True or False. Write the letter ***T*** *in the blank if the sentence is true. Write the letter* ***F*** *in the blank if the sentence is false.*

______16. Mercury made a lyre from a tortoise shell for Apollo.
______17. Cupid carried some bows and one arrow.
______18. Minerva gave an olive tree to the city of Athens.
______19. Apollo's son was the god of medicine.
______20. Venus married Cupid because she fell in love.

THE SOLAR SYSTEM AND THE PLANETS

GLOSSARY

1.	asteroid	a large natural object that is made of metal and rock, is smaller than a planet, and revolves around the Sun
2.	astronomers	scientists who study the sky
3.	clever	tricky; smart
4.	comet	an object that is made of ice and rock, is smaller than a planet, may have a tail of gas and dust, and revolves around the Sun
5.	companions	friends
6.	craters	cup-shaped holes in the land
7.	create (created)	to make
8.	extremely	very
9.	fossils	shapes of animals and plants from long ago found in rocks
10.	grace (graceful)	beautiful or lovely movement
11.	helmet	a kind of hat
12.	language	spoken or written or signed words
13.	locate (located)	to find
14.	meteroid	a natural object that is made of metal and rock, is smaller than an asteroid, and revolves around the Sun
15.	oxygen	the air people and animals breathe
16.	rotate	to turn
17.	sandals	a type of shoes
18.	satellite	a natural or man-made object that revolves around a planet
19.	surface	the top area

OUR GALAXY AND OUR SOLAR SYSTEM

Our solar system was created many, many years ago. It includes the Sun, the planets and their satellites, comets, asteroids, and meteoroids. The names of the nine planets in our solar system are Mercury, Venus, Earth, Mars, Jupiter, Saturn, Uranus, Neptune, and Pluto. Our planet is Earth. Our solar system is very large.

Our Sun is really a star. A star is an object in space that shines from its own energy. The Sun is in the middle of our solar system and it is the only star in our solar system. The nine planets revolve around the Sun. Each planet is a different size. Most of the planets have moons that revolve around them.

Our solar system is located in a galaxy. Our galaxy is called the Milky Way. It incudes our solar system, some other stars with their planets, and millions of other stars that do not have planets. There are many other galaxies and many other stars in space.

Scientists often study about our galaxy and our solar system. Sometimes they send spacecraft into the sky to take pictures. Sometimes they use telescopes to look at objects in our solar system, our galaxy, and even far beyond our galaxy.

Many people, animals, and plants live on our planet Earth. The Earth has one satellite called the Moon. The name "Earth" is not copied from Greek or Roman mythology. The names of the other eight planets are copied from Greek and Roman mythology. Scientists have gathered much information about the Earth. They know some information about the other eight planets, but they want to gather more.

People on Earth can see most of the other planets in our solar system in the sky at night. People can also see many stars. Some of them are in our galaxy, but many of them are not. They are very, very far away.

MERCURY

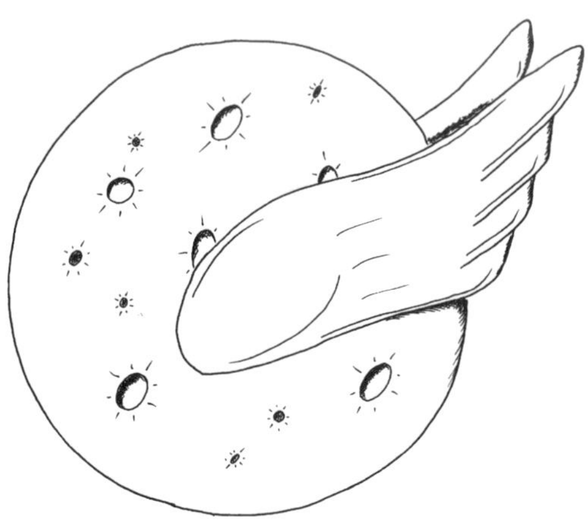

Mercury is the closest planet to the Sun in our solar system. It is also one of the smallest planets. Mercury was once visited by a spacecraft from Earth, named the Mariner. Since Mercury is very close to the Sun it was not safe for the spacecraft to stay very long. It could not take many pictures of the planet to share with the people on Earth.

In Roman mythology, Mercury was the messenger of the gods and goddesses. The god Mercury had great speed and grace. He often traveled around the world to visit different gods and goddesses. He delivered messages to them. Mercury had wings on his hat and his sandals to help him travel more quickly. He also carried a caduceus, a magic staff with wings on the top and two snakes twisted together around it. People believe the planet Mercury was named after the god, Mercury, because the planet moves so quickly in the sky. Astronomers have nicknamed it "The Winged Messenger."

Mercury is a very, very hot planet, but astronomers think there is a north pole on it. They believe it could have ice because the north pole area is often shaded from the Sun. Mercury is a very old planet. Like the Earth's Moon, the surface of Mercury has many craters and some smooth plains. Scientists believe the land on Mercury was formed by volcanoes.

VENUS

Venus is the second planet from the Sun. It is only a little smaller than Earth. Venus was visited by over 20 spacecraft from Earth. Photographs were taken from the spacecraft so maps could be made about Venus. The information collected by the spacecraft helps scientists learn more about Venus.

In Roman mythology, Venus was the goddess of love and beauty. Venus was a very popular goddess. Wherever she walked, flowers bloomed and small birds flew around her. Her favorite bird was the dove. Swans often surrounded her. She was graceful and beautiful like the swans. The swan is often used as a symbol for grace and beauty. People believed that without Venus there would be no joy or peace on Earth.

Astronomers have nicknamed the planet Venus "The Bringer of Peace." People believe that the planet Venus was named after this goddess because it is the brightest planet.

Earth and Venus are very similar. They are about the same size and have similar land areas. They are called "sister planets." Scientists discovered that Venus is a very dry planet. Venus has many clouds surrounding it. There are strong winds near the clouds. Venus still has active volcanoes. The Sun and the Moon are the only objects seen in the sky that are brighter than the planet Venus.

EARTH

Earth is the third planet from the Sun. Scientists believe Earth is very old. The fossils found on Earth help to explain Earth's age. Scientists have taken many pictures of Earth and developed maps. The pictures are used to study more about the Earth. They help in finding out about the weather. They also help show the changes on the land.

Earth is the only planet whose name was not copied from Greek and Roman mythology. The name was copied from the German language. In Roman mythology, the goddess of the Earth was named Tellus. Tellus means "fertile soil" or "Mother Earth."

There are seven continents and several oceans on Earth. The land areas include volcanoes, mountains, valleys, and canyons. There are rivers and seas, too. The temperatures on Earth allow people, animals, and plants to live there. The oxygen on Earth is very important to living things.

Earth has one natural satellite, called the Moon. It takes the Moon about 27 days to revolve around the Earth. The Earth itself turns all the way around every day. That is why places on Earth face the Moon part of the day and are hidden from the Moon the other part of the day.

MARS

Mars is the fourth planet from the Sun in our solar system. It is smaller than the Earth. Mars was visited often by spacecraft from Earth. People on Earth continue to send spacecraft to Mars to gather information. Scientists want to study more about Mars to see if anyone can live there.

In Roman mythology, Mars was the god of war. Mars was not a popular god. The people feared him because he enjoyed war. When Mars fought in a war, he was cruel and unfair. The people thought he was a rude god. A vulture and a mean wolf were his companions. Astronomers have nicknamed the planet Mars "The Bringer of War." People believe the planet was named after the god Mars because it glows in the night sky with a red color. They believe the red color represents the blood from all of the wars that Mars started. People sometimes call it "The Red Planet."

Scientists believe that the land on Mars is similar to the Earth and the Moon. There are mountains, plains, canyons, and valleys found on Mars. Long ago, there were lakes and oceans. The weather on Mars is always cold. There is ice found on both poles. There are often strong winds and huge dust storms that continue for many months. Mars can easily be seen at night because it is a very bright planet.

JUPITER

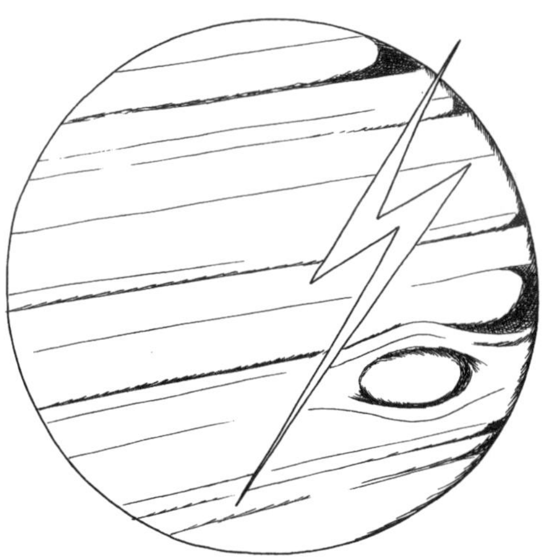

Jupiter is the fifth planet from the Sun and the largest of all the planets. It was visited six different times by spacecraft from the Earth. Scientists often study about the planet Jupiter and its moons.

In Roman mythology, Jupiter was the king of the gods and goddesses. He was the brother of Pluto and Neptune and his father was Saturn. He was the greatest and most powerful of all the gods and goddesses. Jupiter was a clever god. The people both loved and feared him. When Jupiter was angry, he would cause great thunder and lightening storms to occur. People believe that the planet was named after the god Jupiter because of its size and powerful storms.

Jupiter is a very bright planet made of gas and rocks. It is covered with clouds of many colors. It has enormous storms with high winds. One area, called "The Great Red Spot," is a giant storm that has continued for over 300 years. Jupiter has sixteen moons which revolve around it and several dark rings which surround it. One of the largest moons is named Io. In mythology, Io was the name of a woman Jupiter liked very much. Jupiter's wife became very jealous and punished Io.

SATURN

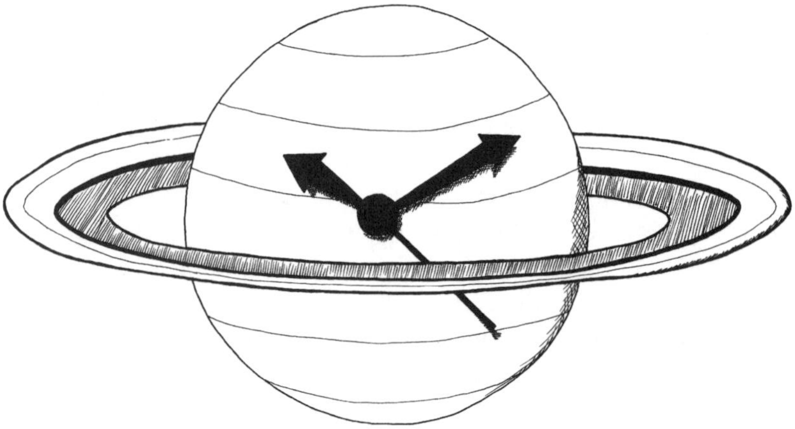

Saturn is the sixth planet from the Sun. It is the second largest planet in our solar system. Saturn was visited by three spacecraft from Earth. A fourth spacecraft, named Cassini, will arrive in the year 2004. This spacecraft was named after a scientist who discovered the moons of Saturn.

In Roman mythology, Saturn was the god of agriculture and the god of time. Saturn was also one of the oldest gods. Saturn was a very mean father who often tried to control his six children. People believe that the planet was named after the god Saturn. Scientists nicknamed the planet "The Bringer of Old Age" because Saturn was the god of time. People believe that Saturday was also named for Saturn.

Saturn has many rings that surround it. Scientists do not know how the rings formed. Scientists think the rings are made of ice and rock. The rings are thin and very bright. Saturn is a hot planet with many storms on it. There are also some areas that are icy. Saturn has more than eighteen moons. They are named after characters in mythology. One of the moons is named for Rhea, Saturn's wife. Rhea was the goddess of the universe. Some of the other moons are named Janus, Pan, Atlas, Prometheus, Epimetheus, and Pandora.

URANUS

Uranus is the seventh planet from the Sun and one of the largest planets. It is larger than Neptune, but smaller than Jupiter and Saturn. Uranus was visited by only one spacecraft from Earth. It is difficult for scientists to study Uranus because they do not have many pictures. They have not collected much information about this planet.

In Greek mythology, Uranus was the god of the heavens. He was the father of Saturn. The Greek people thought Uranus was the most important god. They liked Uranus very much. They believed he had more power than any other god or goddess. Scientists nicknamed the planet "The Magician." People think that the planet was named after the god Uranus because it has a blue color like the heavens.

Scientists have counted eleven dark rings around Uranus. Scientists think the rings are made of rocks and dust. Uranus also has many clouds that surround it. These cause very strong winds on the land. Scientists think that Uranus has about 20 moons that revolve around it. Their names are not copied from mythology.

NEPTUNE

Neptune is the eighth planet from the Sun and one of the largest planets. Only one spacecraft from Earth has ever visited this planet. Scientists do not know very much about Neptune because it is so far away. They nicknamed it "The Mystic."

In Roman mythology, Neptune was the god of the sea. The people believed he lived in a golden palace where he ruled everything in the oceans. They thought he controlled the sea animals and the waves. The people loved the ocean, so they loved Neptune very much. They believed that when Neptune became angry, he caused terrible storms at sea. Like the oceans, the planet Neptune has a blue color. People believe the planet was named for the god of the sea because of the blue color and because it is far away.

The planet Neptune is made of rock and ice. It has the strongest winds of all the planets. Often there are huge storms on this planet. Neptune is surrounded by very dark rings. It also has eight moons. The names of the moons are copied from mythology.

PLUTO

Pluto is the farthest planet from the Sun and the smallest planet. It is smaller than Earth's moon. Pluto was never visited by any spacecraft from Earth. It is difficult for scientists to gather information about Pluto. It is very far from Earth. It takes a very long time for a spacecraft to travel to this planet.

In Roman mythology, Pluto was the god of the underworld. He lived in Hades where it was very dark. Hades was far away from the place where the other gods and goddesses lived. No one visited Hades. It was a place for the dead. Pluto was not a friendly god so many people were afraid of him. Pluto had a helmet that made him invisible when he wore it. People believe the planet was named after the god Pluto because it is a dark planet and it is hard to see.

Pluto is a very cold and dark planet. There is a lot of ice on Pluto because the Sun cannot warm the planet. The land on Pluto is frozen most of the time. There is not much light on Pluto because the light from the Sun is so far away.

Pluto has one moon. It is larger than the Earth's moon and it is named Charon. In Roman mythology, Charon was the name of the character who brought the dead people into the underworld. Mercury took the dead from the earth to Charon, and then Charon took them by boat across the River Styx into Hades. He would leave the dead in the underworld where Pluto lived.

THE SOLAR SYSTEM AND THE PLANETS
STUDY QUESTIONS

Read the questions below. Write the correct answer in each blank.

1. The planet ________________ was nicknamed "The Bringer of Peace."
2. Astronomers nicknamed the planet Mercury ________________.
3. People call the planet Mars ________________ because of its color.
4. Our galaxy is called the ________________.
5. ________________ is the largest planet.
6. ________________ is the smallest planet.
7. The planet ________________ was named for the Greek god of the heavens.
8. The planet ________________ has the strongest winds of all planets.
9. The god Mercury carried a magic staff called a ________________.
10. We use ________________ to see objects in our galaxy and beyond.
11. ________________ is the third planet from the Sun.
12. There are ________________ planets that revolve around the Sun.
13. The planet Saturn and the day Saturday were named for the god of ________________ and ________________.
14. One of the largest moons that revolve around Jupiter is named ________________.
15. ________________ is the closest planet to the Sun.
16. The planet ________________ was named after a beautiful goddess and is the brightest planet.
17. The planet ________________ has a storm that is over 300 years old called "The Great Red Spot."
18. One of the moons of Saturn is named for the goddess of the universe, ________________.
19. The ________________ is the only star in our solar system.
20. The planet Uranus is nicknamed ________________.
21. The planet ________________ has dark rings and eight moons.
22. The planet Pluto was named for the god of ________________.
23. ________________ revolve around planets and can be natural or man-made.
24. Our galaxy includes our solar system, other planets, and millions of ________________.
25. Our ________________ includes planets, the Sun, satellites, comets, asteroids, and meteroids.

USING YOUR RESOURCES

Resources are people and things that help you do something, get information, or answer questions. Your teacher, other students, and the sections of this book are resources that might help you do the following activities. You can talk with your teacher and classmates, look at pictures in this book, or read stories and lists in this book to help you fill in the blanks, label and draw pictures, and answer the questions in the sections that follow. GOOD LUCK!

SOLAR SYSTEM GRAPHIC

Read the sentences below and fill in the names of the objects the sentences describe. Then look at the picture of the solar system on page 161, and label the nine planets and one star with the correct names.

1. This star is in the middle of the solar system. Mercury is the closest planet to this star.
   ____
2. This planet is the largest in the solar system and is named after the king of the gods and goddesses. It is the fifth planet from the Sun. ____________________
3. This planet is the farthest from the Sun and is named after the god of the underworld.
   ____
4. This planet is not named after a Greek or Roman god or goddess. It is our planet and it is the third planet from the Sun. _________________
5. This planet has rings around it. It is named after the god of time and agriculture. _________________
6. This planet is closest to the Sun and is named after the god of speed. ___________________
7. This planet is next to Pluto and it is the eighth planet from the Sun. It is named after the god of the sea.
   ____
8. This planet is between Mercury and Earth. It is named after the goddess of love and beauty.
   ____
9. This planet is between Saturn and Neptune. It is named after Saturn's father. He was the Greek god of the heavens. _______________________
10. This planet is between Earth and Jupiter. It is the fourth planet from the Sun and is named after the god of war. ________________________

Our Solar System

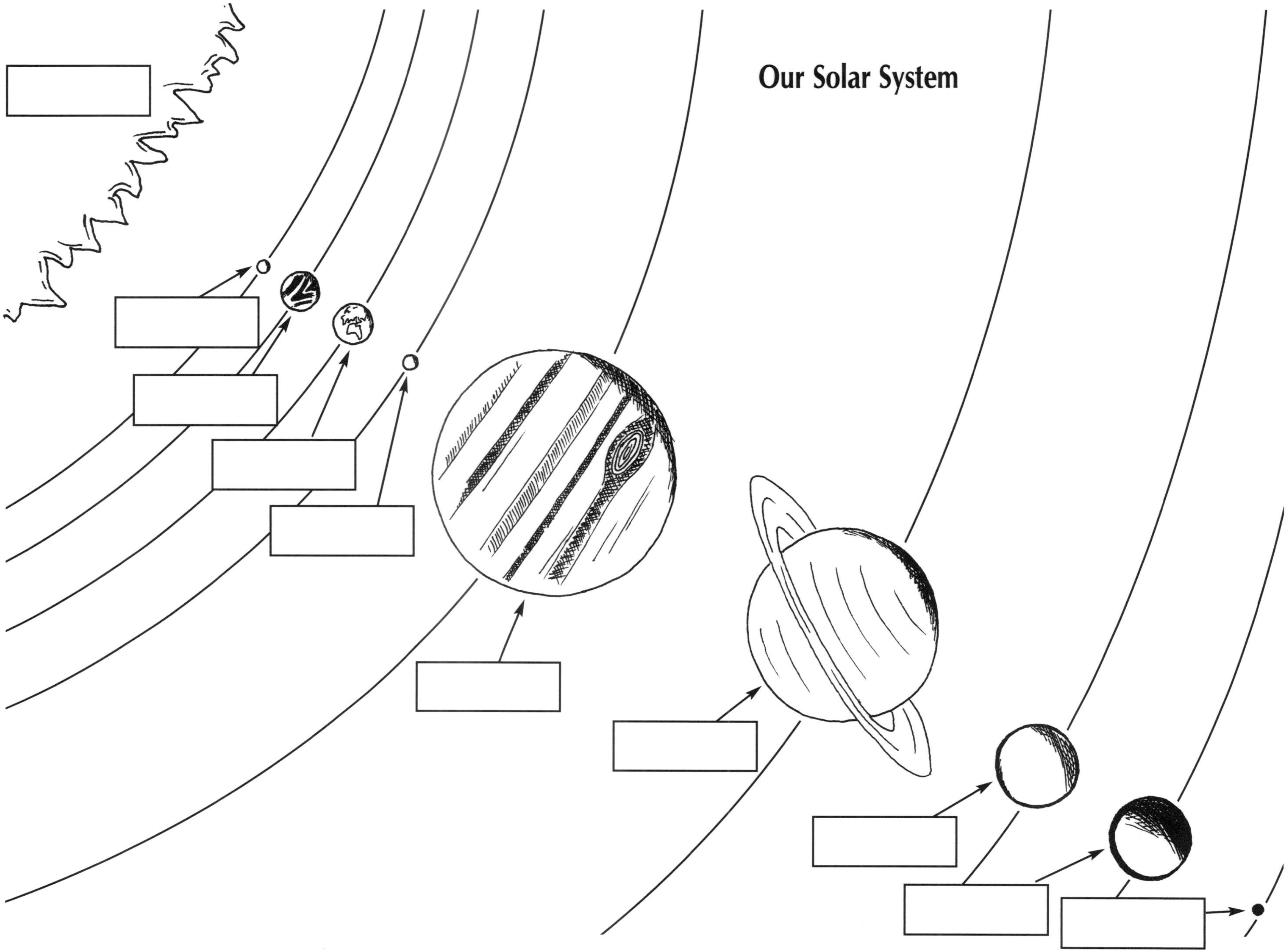

PLANETS, GODS AND GODDESSES, AND SYMBOLS

Look at the pictures of the planets that go with the stories about the planets. The illustrator drew symbols with eight of the planets. These symbols represent the Greek and Roman gods and goddesses whose names were copied and used for the planets.

Use all of your resources to answer the questions. YOU CAN DO IT!

1. A ______________________ is a picture that represents something.

2. *Find the picture of the planet Mercury.*

   a. What symbol did the illustrator draw to represent the god Mercury? ____________________

   b. *Check each answer that correctly completes the sentence.*

   The illustrator may have used this symbol because______________________.
   ____ 1) the planet was named after Mercury, the god of speed
   ____ 2) the planet was named after Mercury, who had wings on his sandals and on his cap
   ____ 3) the planet was named after Mercury, who had wings on his back

   c. Do you think there is another symbol that could represent the god Mercury? ____________
   If you answered "Yes," draw your picture of the symbol below.

3. *Find the picture of the planet Jupiter.*

   a. What symbol did the illustrator draw to represent the god Jupiter? ____________________

   b. *Check each answer that correctly completes the sentence.*

   The illustrator may have used this symbol because________________________.
   ____ 1) a bolt of lightning is a symbol for Jupiter, the king of the gods and goddesses
   ____ 2) this planet was named after Jupiter, the god of storms
   ____ 3) the god Jupiter used lightning as a weapon

c. Do you think there is another symbol that could represent the god Jupiter? ____________
If you answered "Yes," draw your picture of the symbol below.

4. *Find the picture of the planet Saturn.*

a. What symbol did the illustrator draw to represent the god Saturn? ______________________

b. *Check each answer that correctly completes the sentence.*

The illustrator may have used this symbol because ______________________.

____ 1) the planet was named after Saturn, the god of time
____ 2) the hands of a clock represent old people
____ 3) the hands of a clock represent time

c. Do you think there is another symbol that could represent the god Saturn? ____________
If you answered "Yes," draw your picture of the symbol below.

5. *Find the picture of the planet Neptune.*

a. What symbols did the illustrator draw to represent the god Neptune? ____________________

b. *Check each answer that correctly completes the sentence.*

The illustrator may have used these symbols because____________________.

____ 1) the planet was named after Neptune, the god of war
____ 2) the planet was named after Neptune, the god of the sea
____ 3) the planet was named after Neptune who lived in the ocean and carried a trident

c. Do you think there is another symbol that could represent the god Neptune? ______________
If you answered "Yes," draw your picture of the symbol below.

6. *Find the picture of the planet Uranus.*

a. What symbol did the illustrator draw to represent the god Uranus?____________________

b. *Check each answer that correctly completes the sentence.*

The illustrator may have used this symbol because ____________________.

____ 1) the planet was named after Uranus, the god of the heavens
____ 2) this symbol represents the heavens
____ 3) clouds represent bad weather

c. Do you think there is another symbol that could represent the god Uranus? ______________
If you answered "Yes," draw your picture of the symbol below.

7. *Find the picture of the planet Mars.*

a. What symbol did the illustrator draw to represent the god Mars? ____________________

b. *Check each answer that correctly completes the sentence.*

The illustrator may have used this symbol because________________________.

____ 1) this bird and a wolf were the companions of the god Mars
____ 2) this bird is one symbol for Mars, the god of animals
____ 3) this bird is one symbol for Mars, the god of war

c. Do you think there is another symbol that could represent the god Mars? _________________
If you answered "Yes," draw your picture of the symbol below.

8. *Find the picture of the planet Pluto.*

   a. What symbol did the illustrator draw to represent the god Pluto? ______________________

   b. *Check each answer that correctly completes the sentence.*

   The illustrator may have used this symbol because______________________.
   ____ 1) this planet was named after Pluto, the king of the gods and goddesses
   ____ 2) this symbol represents a king
   ____ 3) this planet was named after Pluto, the king of the underworld

   c. Do you think there is another symbol that could represent the god Pluto? ______________________
   If you answered "Yes," draw a picture of the symbol below.

9. *Find the picture of the planet Venus.*

   a. What symbol did the illustrator draw to represent Venus? ______________________

   b. *Check each answer that correctly completes the sentence.*

   The illustrator may have used this symbol because______________________.
   ____ 1) this bird is often used as a symbol for grace and beauty
   ____ 2) the planet was named after Venus, the goddess of love and beauty, who was often surrounded by many of these birds
   ____ 3) the planet was named after Venus, the goddess of birds

c. Do you think there is another symbol that could represent the goddess Venus? _______________
If you answered "Yes," draw your picture of the symbol below.

10. *Find the picture of the planet Earth.*

a. *Check each answer that correctly completes the sentence.*

The illustrator did not draw any symbols with this planet because ________________________.

____ 1) the planet Earth was not named after a Greek or Roman god or goddess
____ 2) the god Earth did not like anything
____ 3) the planet Earth was named after the god of volcanoes and the ocean

b. *The illustrator drew pictures of land areas on the planet Earth. Check the names of two continents that you see.*

____ 1) Europe
____ 2) South America
____ 3) Asia
____ 4) North America
____ 5) Africa

ENRICHMENT ACTIVITIES

1. Interview a florist who is a member of the Florists' Transworld Delivery.

2. Construct a symbol using paper, wood, or any other materials.

3. Create a three-dimensional solar system using a variety of materials.

4. Create your own advertisement, including the name of your product, the name of your own business, a picture of your symbol, and a slogan.

5. Select a symbol that you like. Write a letter to find out more information about that symbol.

6. Choose one planet and write a haiku or poem about it using the information you have learned.

7. Write a short research paper about the Olympic Games and their symbol, the Olympic Rings.

8. Choose a planet and write a research paper that includes information not found in this book. Then make a presention of this information to your class.

9. Choose a symbol. Imagine you are that symbol. Write a paper to describe yourself and to explain how you feel.

10. Write to the United Nations and request information to share with the class.

11. Create an advertisement poster for a trip into space. Include descriptions of what may be seen or visited.

12. Obtain a telephone directory and write a list of companies or businesses that use mythological names or symbols for their products.

13. Find the names of the gods or goddesses from whom we copied the names of the days of the week. Explain what each god or goddess controlled and the reasons the name was used.

14. The following expressions contain mythological references: "Wise as an owl," "By Jove!" "It's hotter than Hades," and "That's a real Pandora's box." Tell what each expression means and explain its mythological reference.

15. Research the scientific reason for an echo and share your findings with the class.

16. The following words were developed from words in mythology: *psychology, panic, chronology, volcano,* and *martial*. Tell what each word means and explain its mythological source.

17. Study the constellations and write about some of the mythological characters associated with them.

18. Collect symbols used in advertisements. Make a collage of the symbols you find.

19. Create a class newspaper with information about mythological references. Share the newspaper with other classes.

20. Visit an observatory and gather information about the research and study of our galaxy. Share this information with the class either in a presentation or on a bulletin board.

ANSWER KEY

SECTION I

Greek and Roman Beliefs and Mount Olympus

1. b
2. c
3. a
4. a
5. b
6. c
7. a
8. c
9. b
10. a

List of Gods and Goddesses

1. Roman
2. Greek
3. Roman, Greek
4. Greek
5. Roman
6. Roman
7. Greek, Roman
8. Roman
9. Greek, Roman
10. Roman
11. Roman, Greek
12. Roman
13. Roman, Greek
14. Greek, Roman
15. Roman
16. Greek
17. Greek, Roman or Roman, Greek

Important Gods and Goddesses

1. a
2. c
3. b
4. b
5. c
6. c
7. a
8. b
9. b
10. a
11. a
12. c
13. c
14. b
15. a
16. b
17. a
18. b
19. c
20. a
21. c
22. a
23. c
24. a
25. c

Crossword Puzzle

Down
1. Pluto
2. Juno
3. Diana
4. Proserpina
5. Hercules
6. Venus
7. Ceres
8. Jupiter
9. Bacchus
10. Juventas

Across
1. Cupid
2. Apollo
3. Mars
4. Saturn
5. Mercury
6. Vesta
7. Neptune
8. Vulcan
9. Minerva

SECTION II

The First Frogs

1. c
2. d
3. b
4. a
5. f
6. frogs
7. muddy
8. gods and goddesses
9. earth
10. swallowed
11. Latona, gods, goddesses, boys
12. woman
13. humans
14. 3 - 4 - 1 - 5 - 2
15. They made the earth shake.
16. They threw rocks at her.
17. They made her go away.
18. They changed them into frogs.
19.
20. ✔
21. ✔
22. ✔
23.
24. ✔
25. because she did something bad
26. to get a drink
27. to make the water muddy
28. because they pitied her
29. because they were awful
30.
31. ✔
32. ✔
33. ✔
34. ✔
35.

The Laurel Tree

1. e
2. d
3. f
4. a
5. b
6. arrows
7. goddess
8. chase
9. trick
10. handsome
11. Cupid, Apollo, Venus, Daphne
12. gods
13. woman
14. 2 - 4 - 5 - 1 - 3
15. He made a laurel wreath.
16. He shot arrows at them.
17. They changed her into a laurel tree.
18. He began to chase her.

19. ✔
20. ✔
21.
22. ✔
23.
24. ✔
25. because he loved her
26. to make a wreath
27. because she was afraid
28. to play a trick on them
29. to help her
30. ✔
31. ✔
32.
33.
34. ✔
35. ✔

The Six Pomegranate Seeds

1. f
2. d
3. b
4. a
5. e
6. months
7. plants
8. seeds
9. Hades
10. earth
11. Mercury, Proserpina, Ceres, Pluto
12. gods
13. goddesses
14. 3 - 4 - 1 - 5 - 2
15. He looked for a queen.
16. She ate six pomegranate seeds.
17. He made an agreement with Pluto.
18. She took care of the plants.
19. ✔
20.
21. ✔
22.
23. ✔
24. ✔
25. because she was sad
26. because Ceres took care of the plants
27. to be his queen
28. because she ate six pomegranate seeds
29. to talk with Pluto
30. ✔
31.
32.
33. ✔
34.
35. ✔

Narcissus

1. d
2. c
3. f
4. b
5. a
6. drink
7. mirror
8. ignored
9. flower
10. handsome
11. Narcissus, maidens
12. boy
13. girls
14. 2 - 4 - 5 - 1 - 3
15. They changed him into a flower.
16. He ignored them.
17. He saw his reflection.
18. He loved it.
19. ✔
20.
21. ✔
22. ✔
23.
24. ✔
25. because they loved him
26. because he did not have a mirror
27. because it was not real
28. because he did not eat and became depressed
29. to get a drink
30. ✔
31.
32. ✔
33.
34. ✔
35.

Pandora

1. c
2. d
3. f
4. e
5. b
6. hope
7. healthy
8. gift
9. fairy
10. problems
11. Pandora, Mercury
12. woman
13. god
14. 2 - 5 - 1 - 4 - 3
15. She opened it.
16. She kissed them and made them feel better.
17. They stung them.
18. He gave it to Pandora.
19.
20.
21.
22. ✔
23. ✔
24. ✔
25. because she was curious
26. to make them feel better
27. because the evil things hurt her
28. because they did not have any problems on earth
29. to give a box to Pandora
30. ✔
31. ✔
32. ✔
33. ✔
34.
35.

Evaluation - Section II

Part I - Characters

1. m
2. c
3. g
4. l
5. h
6. j

7. e
8. k
9. d
10. a
11. i
12. f

Part II - Nouns

13. stones
14. pond
15. pomegranate
16. hunger
17. wreath
18. seasons
19. king
20. maiden
21. bow
22. earth
23. agreement
24. branch
25. arrows
26. seeds
27. frogs

Part III - Verbs

28. b
29. c
30. c
31. b
32. a
33. c
34. c
35. b
36. a
37. c
38. c
39. a
40. b

Part IV - Adjectives

41. depressed
42. six
43. handsome
44. webbed
45. terrible
46. quiet
47. angry
48. muddy
49. favorite
50. special
51. frightened
52. healthy
53. beautiful
54. thirsty
55. fat

Part V - Sequence

56. 3 - 1 - 4 - 2
57. 4 - 2 - 3 - 1
58. 2 - 3 - 4 - 1
59. 2 - 4 - 1 - 3
60. 4 - 2 - 3 - 1

Part VI - Greek and Roman Beliefs

61.
62. ✔
63. ✔
64. ✔
65.
66.
67. ✔
68.
69. ✔
70.

SECTION III

Daedalus and Icarus

1. b
2. e
3. f
4. a
5. d
6. wax
7. arms
8. ignored
9. feathers
10. escape
11. King Minos, Daedalus, Icarus
12. son
13. inventor
14. 4 - 2 - 5 - 1 - 3
15. They tied them to their arms.
16. He made many things.
17. He made wings.
18. He put him in a tower on an island.
19. ✔
20.
21. ✔
22. ✔
23.
24.
25. to make wings
26. because Icarus flew near the sun
27. to escape from the island
28. because he was angry
29. because he ignored his father
30. ✔
31.
32. ✔
33.
34.
35. ✔

Prometheus and the Fire

1. b
2. e
3. c
4. a
5. d
6. permission
7. rock
8. suffer
9. chains
10. fur
11. Prometheus, Hercules, Jupiter, Epimetheus
12. giants
13. god
14. 3 - 1 - 5 - 4 - 2
15. He lit a torch with fire from the sun.
16. He punished him.
17. They came to peck at his body.
18. He broke the chains.
19. ✔
20. ✔
21.
22. ✔
23. ✔
24.

25. to help people on earth
26. to peck at his body
27. because they thought fire was a wonderful gift
28. because he stole fire from the sun
29. to get fire
30. ✔
31. ✔
32.
33.
34. ✔
35. ✔

Hyacinthus

1. b
2. f
3. c
4. e
5. a
6. plant
7. horseshoe
8. jealous
9. bloomed
10. friend
11. Hyacinthus, Apollo, Zephyrus
12. boy
13. god
14. 2 - 5 - 3 - 4 - 1
15. They played horseshoes.
16. They named it.
17. He blew a horseshoe at Hyacinthus.
18. He fell into a flower bed and died.
19.
20. ✔
21.
22.
23. ✔
24. ✔
25. because Apollo and Hyacinthus played together
26. because the horseshoe hit his head
27. because he was jealous
28. to remember Hyacinthus
29. because his friend died
30. ✔
31. ✔
32. ✔
33.
34. ✔
35.

Iris

1. f
2. e
3. d
4. a
5. b
6. rainbow
7. colors
8. end
9. visit
10. meeting
11. Apollo, Neptune, Iris
12. gods
13. daughter
14. 1 - 3 - 5 - 2 - 4
15. He made a beautiful bridge.
16. She went to visit her favorite gods and goddesses.
17. She took messages to other gods and goddesses.
18. They planned to build a bridge for Iris.
19. ✔
20. ✔
21.
22.
23.
24.
25. because that was his favorite color
26. to talk to Neptune
27. to talk about Iris
28. because it was beautiful
29. to visit her favorite gods and goddesses
30. ✔
31. ✔
32. ✔
33. ✔
34.
35.

Aurora and Tithonus

1. e
2. a
3. c
4. f
5. d
6. uncomfortable
7. begged
8. pale
9. meadow
10. wrinkled
11. Aurora, Jupiter, Tithonus
12. goddess
13. boy
14. 2 - 5 - 1 - 4 - 3
15. He changed him into an old man.
16. He begged Aurora to help him.
17. She changed him into a grasshopper.
18. He slept in the meadow.
19. ✔
20.
21.
22. ✔
23. ✔
24. ✔
25. because he was uncomfortable
26. to ask Jupiter for help
27. because he became an old man
28. to wake up the flowers and animals
29. because he wanted to see Aurora each morning
30. ✔
31. ✔
32. ✔
33.
34.
35.

Evaluation - Section III

Part I - Characters

1. d
2. h
3. l
4. j
5. a
6. k

7. b
8. c
9. m
10. g
11. i
12. f

Part II - Nouns

13. meadow
14. bridge
15. torch
16. grasshopper
17. inventor
18. horseshoe
19. giants
20. dawn
21. rainbow
22. feathers
23. earth
24. island
25. flower
26. fire
27. chains

Part III - Verbs

28. b
29. b
30. c
31. c
32. b
33. a
34. b
35. c
36. a
37. a
38. b
39. c
40. b

Part IV - Adjectives

41. pale
42. jealous
43. green
44. young
45. wise
46. strong
47. sad
48. large
49. sharp
50. dry
51. beautiful
52. charming
53. cold
54. mean
55. favorite

Part V - Sequence

56. 2 - 4 - 1 - 3
57. 4 - 2 - 1 - 3
58. 2 - 4 - 3 - 1
59. 2 - 4 - 1 - 3
60. 3 - 4 - 1 - 2

Part VI - Greek and Roman Beliefs

61. ✔
62.
63. ✔
64. ✔
65.
66. ✔
67. ✔
68. ✔
69.
70.

SECTION IV

Pegasus and Bellerophon

1. d
2. f
3. b
4. a
5. c
6. hero
7. conquer
8. fell
9. curious
10. agreed
11. Minerva, king, Bellerophon, Pegasus
12. goddess
13. man
14. e
15. a
16. b
17. d
18. e
19. a
20. c
21. b
22. d
23. 4 - 1 - 5 - 2 - 3
24.
25. ✔
26.
27. ✔
28. ✔
29.
30.
31. ✔
32.
33. ✔
34. ✔
35.

Minerva and Arachne

1. d
2. a
3. b
4. e
5. f
6. designs
7. looms
8. mocked
9. contest
10. wrinkled
11. people, Minerva, Arachne, animals
12. woman
13. goddess
14. b
15. d
16. a
17. e
18. d
19. b
20. e
21. a
22. c
23. 2 - 5 - 3 - 1 - 4
24. ✔
25.
26.
27. ✔
28. ✔
29.
30.
31.

32. ✔
33. ✔
34.
35. ✔

Phaethon

1. e
2. d
3. a
4. f
5. b
6. rear
7. palace
8. reins
9. robes
10. realized
11. Apollo, boys, Jupiter, Phaethon, Clymene
12. god
13. boy
14. e
15. d
16. b
17. a
18. f
19. b
20. e
21. c
22. d
23. 2 - 5 - 4 - 1 - 3
24. ✔
25. ✔
26. ✔
27.
28.
29. ✔
30. ✔
31. ✔
32.
33. ✔
34. ✔
35.

The Hundred-Eyed Argus

1. e
2. b
3. a
4. f
5. c
6. shepherd
7. entire
8. flirted
9. flute
10. sword
11. Mercury, Argus, Juno, Jupiter, Io
12. gods
13. goddess
14. b
15. d
16. a
17. e
18. a
19. d
20. f
21. b
22. c
23. 1 - 4 - 5 - 3 - 2
24. ✔
25.
26. ✔
27.
28.
29. ✔
30.
31. ✔
32. ✔
33.
34.
35. ✔

How the City Was Named

1. f
2. a
3. d
4. e
5. b
6. honor
7. buds
8. fountains
9. capital
10. olive
11. Jupiter, Minerva, Neptune
12. gods
13. goddess
14. c
15. a
16. d
17. e
18. b
19. a
20. e
21. c
22. d
23. 2 - 4 - 1 - 5 - 3
24.
25. ✔
26. ✔
27.
28.
29. ✔
30. ✔
31.
32.
33. ✔
34. ✔
35. ✔

Evaluation - Section IV

Part I - Characters

1. d
2. f
3. a
4. l
5. h
6. j
7. c
8. e
9. g
10. i
11. b
12. m

Part II - Nouns

13. temple
14. capital
15. shepherd
16. throne
17. contest
18. designs
19. weed
20. weaver
21. looms
22. flute
23. hero
24. webs
25. fangs
26. journey
27. bridle

Part III - Verbs

28. c
29. b
30. a
31. c
32. b
33. a
34. b
35. a
36. b
37. c
38. a
39. a
40. b

Part IV - Adjectives

41. curious
42. wrinkled
43. swift
44. depressed
45. famous
46. clever
47. furious
48. weak
49. relaxed
50. fragrant
51. nervous
52. jealous
53. thrilled
54. skillful
55. entire

Part V - Sequence

56. 4 - 2 - 3 - 1
57. 2 - 4 - 3 - 1
58. 2 - 4 - 3 - 1
59. 2 - 4 - 1 - 3
60. 2 - 1 - 3 - 4

Part VI - Greek and Roman Beliefs

61.
62. ✔
63. ✔
64. ✔
65.
66.
67. ✔
68.
69. ✔
70. ✔

SECTION V

Echo and Narcissus

1. c
2. a
3. f
4. d
5. e
6. repeated
7. cave
8. waded
9. weak
10. disappeared
11. Cupid, Echo, Narcissus
12. god
13. woman
14. a
15. e
16. d
17. b
18. d
19. c
20. a
21. e
22. f
23. 1 - 4 - 5 - 3 - 2
24.
25. ✔
26. ✔
27.
28. ✔
29.
30.
31. ✔
32.
33.
34. ✔
35.

Clytie

1. c
2. d
3. b
4. f
5. e
6. roots
7. palace
8. chariot
9. huge
10. coral
11. Clytie
12. nymph
13. goddess
14. b
15. e
16. a
17. d
18. c
19. f
20. a
21. e
22. b
23. 4 - 3 - 1 - 5 - 2
24. ✔
25. ✔
26.
27.
28.
29. ✔
30.
31. ✔
32.
33.
34. ✔
35.

Atlas

1. c
2. f
3. b
4. a
5. d
6. pad
7. muscles
8. shoulders
9. difficult
10. tumble
11. Jupiter, Prometheus, Atlas, Hercules
12. giant
13. women
14. d
15. c
16. a
17. b
18. b

19. d
20. c
21. a
22. e
23. 5 - 3 - 1 - 2 - 4
24.
25.
26.
27. ✔
28.
29. ✔
30. ✔
31.
32. ✔
33. ✔
34.
35.

Orion

1. b
2. e
3. f
4. a
5. d
6. power
7. deep
8. aim
9. target
10. scorpion
11. Orion, Apollo, Diana
12. goddess
13. giant
14. c
15. e
16. a
17. b
18. a
19. f
20. c
21. b
22. e
23. 1 - 3 - 5 - 4 - 2
24. ✔
25. ✔
26.
27. ✔
28. ✔
29. ✔
30. ✔
31.
32. ✔
33. ✔
34.
35.

Saturn

1. c
2. d
3. e
4. b
5. f
6. honor
7. banished
8. offered
9. harvested
10. escaped
11. Jupiter, people, Saturn
12. god
13. god
14. d
15. c
16. b
17. e
18. f
19. d
20. e
21. a
22. b
23. 5 - 1 - 4 - 3 - 2
24. ✔
25.
26. ✔
27.
28. ✔
29. ✔
30. ✔
31. ✔
32.
33.
34.
35.

Evaluation - Section V

Part I - Characters

1. k
2. a
3. f
4. m
5. c
6. b
7. g
8. j
9. d
10. l
11. e
12. h

Part II - Nouns

13. pearls
14. giant
15. scorpion
16. power
17. pad
18. cave
19. celebration
20. behavior
21. dolphins
22. roots
23. muscles
24. surface
25. sweat
26. nymph
27. target

Part III - Verbs

28. a
29. c
30. a
31. b
32. a
33. b
34. c
35. b
36. b
37. a
38. c
39. a
40. b

Part IV - Adjectives

41. deep
42. jealous
43. overjoyed
44. rushing
45. upset
46. sore
47. weak
48. difficult
49. handsome

50. depressed
51. young
52. terrible
53. skillful
54. anxious
55. huge

Part V - Sequence

56. 4 - 2 - 3 - 1
57. 1 - 2 - 4 - 3
58. 2 - 3 - 4 - 1
59. 4 - 2 - 1 - 3
60. 1 - 3 - 2 - 4

Part VI - Greek and Roman Beliefs

61. ✔
62.
63.
64. ✔
65.
66. ✔
67.
68.
69.
70. ✔

SECTION VI

The Months

1. 12 (twelve)
2. Latin
3. June
4. May
5. calendar
6. Janus
7. August
8. February
9. July
10. October
11. nine
12. Aphrodite
13. decem
14. 365
15. September

Symbol Stories

1. d
2. a
3. f
4. c
5. b
6. deliver
7. symbol
8. represent
9. settle
10. conducts
11. physician
12. United Nations
13. musician
14. love
15. F.T.D.
16. T
17. F
18. T
19. T
20. F

The Solar System and the Planets

1. Venus
2. The Winged Messenger
3. The Bringer of War/The Red Planet
4. Milky Way
5. Jupiter
6. Pluto
7. Uranus
8. Neptune
9. caduceus
10. telescopes/spacecraft
11. Earth
12. nine
13. agriculture; time
14. Io
15. Mercury
16. Venus
17. Jupiter
18. Rhea
19. Sun
20. The Magician
21. Neptune
22. the underworld/Hades
23. satellites
24. stars
25. solar system

Solar System Graphic

1. The Sun
2. Jupiter
3. Pluto
4. Earth
5. Saturn
6. Mercury
7. Neptune
8. Venus
9. Uranus
10. Mars

NOTE: see next page for "Our Solar System" graphic answers

Planets, Gods and Goddesses, and Symbols

1. symbol
2. a. wings
   b. 1) ✔
      2) ✔
      3)
   c. (answers will vary)
3. a. lightning bolt
   b. 1) ✔
      2)
      3) ✔
   c. (answers will vary)
4. a. clock/hands of a clock
   b. 1) ✔
      2)
      3) ✔
   c. (answers will vary)
5. a. trident, waves
   b. 1)
      2) ✔
      3) ✔
   c. (answers will vary)
6. a. clouds/the heavens
   b. 1) ✔
      2) ✔
      3)
   c. (answers will vary)
7. a. vulture
   b. 1) ✔
      2)
      3) ✔
   c. (answers will vary)

8. a. crown, black/dark color
   b. 1)
      2) ✔
      3) ✔
   c. (answers will vary)
9. a. swan
   b. 1) ✔
      2) ✔
      3)
   c. (answers will vary)
10. a. 1) ✔
       2)
       3)
    b. 1)
       2) ✔
       3)
       4) ✔
       5)

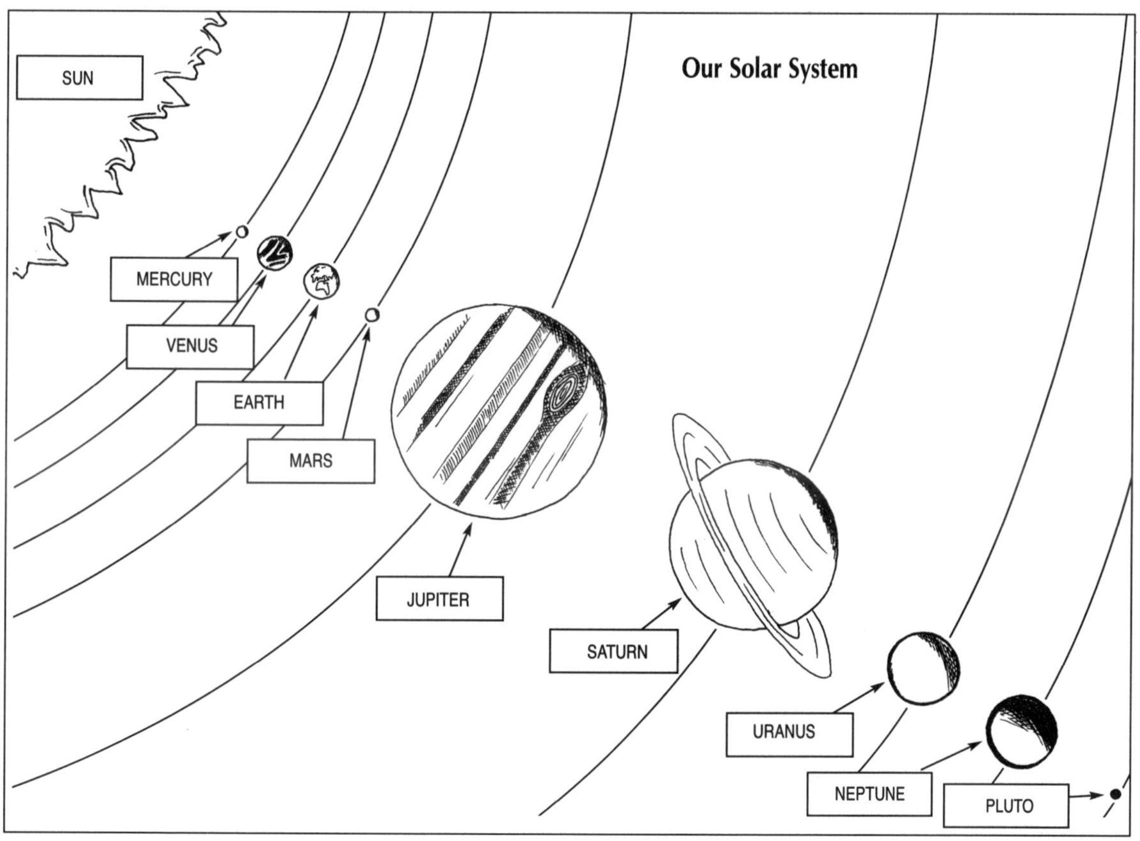